PORNOGRAPHY
AND SO ON

by

D. H. LAWRENCE

Fredonia Books
Amsterdam, The Netherlands

Pornography and So On

by
D. H. Lawrence

ISBN: 1-58963-623-6

Fredonia Books
Amsterdam, The Netherlands
http://www.fredoniabooks.com

CONTENTS

PORNOGRAPHY AND
OBSCENITY

PORNOGRAPHY AND OBSCENITY

What they are depends, as usual, entirely on the individual. What is pornography to one man is the laughter of genius to another.

The word itself, we are told, means 'pertaining to harlots'—the graph of the harlot. But nowadays, what is a harlot? If she was a woman who took money from a man in return for going to bed with him—really, most wives sold themselves, in the past, and plenty of harlots gave themselves, when they felt like it, for nothing. If a woman hasn't got a tiny streak of a harlot in her, she's a dry stick as a rule. And probably most harlots had somewhere a streak of womanly generosity. Why be so cut and dried? The law is a dreary thing, and its judgments have nothing to do with life.

The same with the word *obscene*: nobody knows what it means. Suppose it were derived from *ob-scena*: that which might not be represented on the stage: how much further are you? None! What is obscene to Tom is not obscene to Lucy or Joe, and really, the meaning of a word has to wait for majorities to decide it. If a play shocks ten people in an audience, and doesn't shock the remaining five hundred, then it is obscene to ten and innocuous to five hundred; hence the play is not obscene, by majority. But *Hamlet* shocked all the Cromwellian Puritans, and shocks nobody to-day, and some of Aristophanes shocks everybody to-day, and didn't galvanize the later Greeks at all, apparently. Man is a changeable beast, and words change their meanings with him, and things are not what they seemed, and what's what becomes what isn't, and if we think we know where we are it's only because we are so rapidly being translated to somewhere else. We have to leave everything to the majority, everything to the majority, everything to the mob, the mob, the mob. They know what is obscene and what isn't, they do. If the lower ten million doesn't know better than the upper ten men, then there's something wrong with mathematics. Take a vote on it! Show hands, and prove it by count! Vox populi, vox Dei. Odi profanum vulgus! Profanum vulgus.

So it comes down to this: if you are talking to the mob, the meaning of your words is the mob-meaning, decided by majority. As somebody wrote to me: the American law on obscenity is very plain, and America is going to enforce the law. Quite, my dear, quite, quite, quite! The mob knows all about obscenity. Mild little words that rhyme with spit or farce are the height of obscenity. Supposing a printer put 'h' in the place of 'p', by mistake, in that mere word spit? Then the great American public knows that this man has committed an obscenity, an indecency, that his act was lewd, and as a compositor he was pornographical. You can't tamper with the great public, British or American. Vox populi, vox Dei, don't you know. If you don't we'll let you know it. At the same time, this vox

Dei shouts with praise over moving-pictures and books and newspaper accounts that seem, to a sinful nature like mine, completely disgusting and obscene. Like a real prude and Puritan, I have to look the other way. When obscenity becomes mawkish, which is its palatable form for the public, and when the Vox populi, vox Dei, is hoarse with sentimental indecency, then I have to steer away, like a Pharisee, afraid of being contaminated. There is a certain kind of sticky universal pitch that I refuse to touch.

So again, it comes down to this: you accept the majority, the mob, and its decisions, or you don't. You bow down before the Vox populi, vox Dei, or you plug your ears not to hear its obscene howl. You perform your antics to please the vast public, Deus ex machina, or you refuse to perform for the public at all, unless now and then to pull its elephantine and ignominious leg.

When it comes to the meaning of anything, even the simplest word, then you must pause. Because there are two great categories of meaning, forever separate. There is mob-meaning, and there is individual meaning. Take even the word *bread*. The mob-meaning is merely: stuff made with white flour into loaves that you eat. But take the individual meaning of the word bread: the white, the brown, the corn-pone, the home-made, the smell of bread just out of the oven, the crust, the crumb, the unleavened bread, the shew-bread, the staff of life, sour-dough bread, cottage loaves, French bread, Viennese bread, black bread, a yesterday's loaf, rye, Graham, barley, rolls, Bretzeln, Kringeln, scones, damper, matsen—there is no end to it all, and the word bread will take you to the ends of time and space, and far-off down avenues of memory. But this is individual. The word bread will take the individual off on his own journey, and its meaning will be his own meaning, based on his own genuine imaginative reactions. And when a word comes to us in its individual character, and starts in us the individual responses, it is a great pleasure to us. The American advertisers have discovered this, and some of the cunningest American literature is to be found in advertisements of soapsuds, for example. These

15

advertisements are *almost* prose-poems. They give the word soapsuds a bubbly, shiny individual meaning, which is very skilfully poetic, would, perhaps, be quite poetic to the mind which could forget that the poetry was bait on a hook.

Business is discovering the individual, dynamic meaning of words, and poetry is losing it. Poetry more and more tends to far-fetch its word-meanings, and this results once again in mob-meanings, which arouse only a mob-reaction in the individual. For every man has a mob-self and an individual self, in varying proportions. Some men are almost all mob-self, incapable of imaginative individual responses. The worst specimens of mob-self are usually to be found in the professions, lawyers, professors, clergymen and so on. The business man, much maligned, has a tough outside mob-self, and a scared, floundering, yet still alive individual self. The public, which is feeble-minded like an idiot, will never be able to preserve its individual reactions from the tricks of the exploiter. The public is always exploited and always will be exploited. The methods of exploitation merely vary. To-day the public is tickled into laying the golden egg. With imaginative words and individual meanings it is tricked into giving the great goose-cackle of mob-acquiescence. Vox populi, vox Dei. It has always been so, and will always be so. Why? Because the public has not enough wit to distinguish between mob-meanings and individual meanings. The mass is forever vulgar, because it can't distinguish between its own original feelings and feelings which are diddled into existence by the exploiter. The public is always profane, because it is controlled from the outside, by the trickster, and never from the inside, by its own sincerity. The mob is always obscene, because it is always second-hand.

Which brings us back to our subject of pornography and obscenity. The reaction to any word may be, in any individual, either a mob-reaction or an individual reaction. It is up to the individual to ask himself: Is my reaction individual, or am I merely reacting from my mob-self?

When it comes to the so-called obscene words, I should say that hardly one person in a million escapes mob-reaction. The first reaction is almost sure to be mob-reaction, mob-indignation, mob-condemnation. And the mob gets no further. But the real individual has second thoughts and says: am I really shocked? Do I *really* feel outraged and indignant? And the answer of any individual is bound to be: No, I am not shocked, not outraged, nor indignant. I know the word, and take it for what it is, and I am not going to be jockeyed into making a mountain out of a mole-hill, not for all the law in the world.

Now if the use of a few so-called obscene words will startle man or woman out of a mob-habit into an individual state, well and good. And word prudery is so universal a mob-habit that it is time we were startled out of it.

But still we have only tackled obscenity, and the problem of pornography goes even deeper. When a man is startled into his individual self, he still may not be able to know, inside himself, whether Rabelais is or is not pornographic: and over Aretino or even Boccaccio he may perhaps puzzle in vain, torn between different emotions.

18

One essay on pornography, I remember, comes to the conclusion that pornography in art is that which is calculated to arouse sexual desire, or sexual excitement. And stress is laid on the fact, whether the author or artist *intended* to arouse sexual feelings. It is the old vexed question of intention, become so dull to-day, when we know how strong and influential our unconscious intentions are. And why a man should be held guilty of his conscious intentions, and innocent of his unconscious intentions, I don't know, since every man is more made up of unconscious intentions than of conscious ones. I am what I am, not merely what I think I am.

However! We take it, I assume, that *pornography* is something base, something unpleasant. In short, we don't like it. And why don't we like it? Because it arouses sexual feelings?

I think not. No matter how hard we may pretend otherwise, most of us rather like a moderate rousing of our sex. It warms us, stimulates us like sunshine on a grey day. After a century or two of Puritanism, this is still true of most people. Only the mob-habit of condemning any form of sex is too strong to let us admit it naturally. And there are, of course, many people who are genuinely repelled by the simplest and most natural stirrings of sexual feeling. But these people are perverts who have fallen into hatred of their fellow men: thwarted, disappointed, unfulfilled people, of whom, alas, our civilization contains so many. And they nearly always enjoy some unsimple and unnatural form of sex excitement, secretly.

Even quite advanced art critics would try to make us believe that any picture or book which had 'sex appeal' was *ipso facto* a bad book or picture. This is just canting hypocrisy. Half the great poems, pictures, music, stories of the whole world are great by virtue of the beauty of their sex appeal. Titian or Renoir, the *Song of Solomon* or *Jane Eyre*, Mozart or *Annie Laurie*, the loveliness is all interwoven with sex appeal, sex stimulus, call it what you will. Even Michael Angelo, who rather hated sex, can't help filling the Cornucopia with phallic acorns. Sex is a very powerful, beneficial and necessary stimulus in human life, and we are all grateful when we feel its warm, natural flow through us, like a form of sunshine.

So we can dismiss the idea that sex appeal in art is pornography. It may be so to the grey Puritan, but the grey Puritan is a sick man, soul and body sick, so why should we bother about his hallucinations? Sex appeal, of course, varies enormously. There are endless different kinds, and endless degrees of each kind. Perhaps it may be argued that a mild degree of sex appeal is not pornographical, whereas a high degree is. But this is a fallacy. Boccaccio at his hottest seems to me less pornographical than *Pamela* or *Clarissa Harlowe* or even *Jane Eyre*, or a host of modern books or films which pass uncensored. At the same time Wagner's *Tristan and Isolde* seems to me very near to pornography, and so, even, do some quite popular Christian hymns.

What is it, then? It isn't a question of sex appeal, merely: nor even a question of deliberate intention on the part of the author or artist to arouse sexual excitement. Rabelais sometimes had a deliberate intention, so in a different way did Boccaccio.

And I'm sure poor Charlotte Brontë, or the authoress of *The Sheik* did *not* have any deliberate intention to stimulate sex feelings in the reader. Yet I find *Jane Eyre* verging towards pornography and Boccaccio seems to me always fresh and wholesome.

The late British Home Secretary, who prides himself on being a very sincere Puritan, grey, grey in every fibre, said with indignant sorrow in one of his outbursts on improper books: '—and these two young people, who had been perfectly pure up till that time, after reading this book went and had sexual intercourse together! ! !' *One up to them!* is all we can answer. But the grey Guardian of British Morals seemed to think that if they had murdered one another, or worn each other to rags of nervous prostration, it would have been much better. The grey disease!

Then what is pornography, after all this? It isn't sex appeal or sex stimulus in art. It isn't even a deliberate intention on the part of the artist to arouse or to excite sexual feelings. There's nothing wrong with sexual feelings in themselves, so long as they are straightforward and not sneaking or sly. The right sort of sex stimulus is invaluable to human daily life. Without it the world grows grey. I would give everybody the gay Renaissance stories to read, they would help to shake off a lot of grey self-importance, which is our modern civilized disease.

But even I would censor genuine pornography, rigorously. It would not be very difficult. In the first place, genuine pornography is almost always underworld, it doesn't come into the open. In the second, you can recognize it by the insult it offers, invariably, to sex, and to the human spirit.

Pornography is the attempt to insult sex, to do dirt on it. This is unpardonable. Take the very lowest instance, the picture post-card sold underhand, by the underworld, in most cities. What I have seen of them have been of an ugliness to make you cry. The insult to the human body, the insult to a vital human relationship! Ugly and cheap they make the human nudity, ugly and degraded they make the sexual act, trivial and cheap and nasty.

It is the same with the books they sell in the underworld. They are either so ugly they make you ill, or so fatuous you can't imagine anybody but a cretin or a moron reading them, or writing them.

It is the same with the dirty limericks that people tell after dinner, or the dirty stories one hears commercial travellers telling each other in a smoke-room. Occasionally there is a really funny one, that redeems a great deal. But usually they are just ugly and repellent, and the so-called 'humour' is just a trick of doing dirt on sex.

Now the human nudity of a great many modern people is just ugly and degraded, and the sexual act between modern people is just the same, merely ugly and degrading. But this is nothing to be proud of. It is the catastrophe of our civilization. I am sure no other civilization, not even the Roman, has showed such a vast proportion of ignominious and degraded nudity, and ugly, squalid dirty sex. Because no other civilization has driven sex into the underworld, and nudity to the W.C.

24

The intelligent young, thank heaven, seem determined to alter in these two respects. They are rescuing their young nudity from the stuffy, pornographical hole-and-corner underworld of their elders, and they refuse to sneak about the sexual relation. This is a change the elderly grey ones of course deplore, but it is in fact a very great change for the better, and a real revolution.

But it is amazing how strong is the will in ordinary, vulgar people, to do dirt on sex. It was one of my fond illusions, when I was young, that the ordinary healthy-seeming sort of men, in railway carriages, or the smoke-room of an hotel or a pullman, were healthy in their feelings and had a wholesome rough devil-may-care attitude toward sex. All wrong! All wrong! Experience teaches that common individuals of this sort have a disgusting attitude toward sex, a disgusting contempt of it, a disgusting desire to insult it. If such fellows have intercourse with a woman, they triumphantly feel that they have done her dirt, and now she is lower, cheaper, more contemptible than she was before.

It is individuals of this sort that tell dirty stories, carry indecent picture post-cards, and know the indecent books. This is the great pornographical class—the really common men-in-the-street and women-in-the-street. They have as great a hate and contempt of sex as the greyest Puritan, and when an appeal is made to them, they are always on the side of the angels. They insist that a film-heroine shall be a neuter, a sexless thing of washed-out purity. They insist that real sex-feeling shall only be shown by the villain or villainess, low lust. They find a Titian or a Renoir really indecent, and they don't want their wives and daughters to see it.

Why? Because they have the grey disease of sex-hatred, coupled with the yellow disease of dirt lust. The sex functions and the excrementory functions in the human body work so close together, yet they are, so to speak, utterly different in direction. Sex is a creative flow, the excrementory flow is towards dissolution, de-creation, if we may use such a word. In the really healthy human being the dis-tinction between the two is instant, our profoundest instincts are perhaps our instincts of opposition between the two flows.

But in the degraded human being the deep instincts have gone dead, and then the two flows become identical. *This* is the secret of really vulgar and of pornographical people: the sex flow and the excrement flow is the same thing to them. It happens when the psyche deteriorates, and the profound controlling instincts collapse. Then sex is dirt and dirt is sex, and sexual excitement becomes a playing with dirt, and any sign of sex in a woman becomes a show of her dirt. This is the condition of the common, vulgar human being whose name is legion, and who lifts his voice and it is the Vox populi, vox Dei. And this is the source of all pornography.

And for this reason we must admit that *Jane Eyre* or Wagner's *Tristan* are much nearer to pornography than is Boccaccio. Wagner and Charlotte Brontë were both in the state where the strongest instincts have collapsed, and sex has become something slightly obscene, to be wallowed in, but despised. Mr. Rochester's sex passion is not 'respectable' till Mr. Rochester is burned, blinded, disfigured and reduced to helpless dependence. Then, thoroughly humbled and humiliated, it may be merely admitted. All the previous titillations are slightly indecent, as in *Pamela* or *The Mill on the Floss* or *Anna Karenina*. As soon as there is sex excitement with a desire to spite the sexual feeling, to humiliate it and degrade it, the element of pornography enters.

For this reason, there is an element of pornography in nearly all nineteenth-century literature, and very many so-called pure people have a nasty pornographical side to them, and never was the pornographical appetite stronger than it is to-day. It is a sign of a diseased condition of the body politic. But the way to treat the disease is to come out into the open with sex and sex stimulus. The real pornographer truly dislikes Boccaccio, because the fresh healthy naturalness of the Italian story-teller makes the modern pornographical shrimp feel the dirty worm he is. To-day Boccaccio should be given to everybody young or old, to read if they like. Only a natural fresh openness about sex will do any good, now we are being swamped by secret or semi-secret pornography. And perhaps the Renaissance story-tellers, Boccaccio, Lasca and the rest, are the best antidote we can find now, just as more plasters of Puritanism are the most harmful remedy we can resort to.

The whole question of pornography seems to me a question of secrecy. Without secrecy there would be no pornography. But secrecy and modesty are two utterly different things. Secrecy has always an element of fear in it, amounting very often to hate. Modesty is gentle and reserved. To-day, modesty is thrown to the winds, even in the presence of the grey guardians. But secrecy is hugged, being a vice in itself. And the attitude of the grey ones is: Dear young ladies, you may abandon all modesty, so long as you hug your dirty little secret.

This 'dirty little secret' has become infinitely precious to the mob of people to-day. It is a kind of hidden sore or inflammation which, when rubbed or scratched, gives off sharp thrills that seem delicious. So the dirty little secret is rubbed and scratched more and more, till it becomes more and more secretly inflamed, and the nervous and psychic health of the individual is more and more impaired. One might easily say that half the love-novels and half the love-films to-day depend entirely for their success on the secret rubbing of the dirty little secret. You can call this sex-excitement if you like, but it is sex-excitement of a secretive, furtive sort, quite special. The plain and simple excitement, quite open and wholesome, which you find in some Boccaccio stories is not for a minute to be confused with the furtive excitement aroused by rubbing the dirty little secret in all secrecy in modern best-sellers. This furtive, sneaking, cunning rubbing of an inflamed spot in the imagination is the very quick of modern pornography, and it is a beastly and very dangerous thing. You can't so easily expose it, because of its very furtiveness and its sneaking cunning. So the cheap and popular modern love-novel and love-film flourishes and is even praised by moral guardians, because you get the sneaking thrill fumbling under all the purity of dainty underclothes, without one single gross word to let you know what is happening.

Without secrecy there would be no pornography. But if pornography is the result of sneaking secrecy, what is the result of pornography? What is the effect on the individual?

The effect on the individual is manifold, and always pernicious. But one effect is perhaps inevitable. The pornography of to-day, whether it be the pornography of the rubber-goods shop or the pornography of the popular novel, film and play, is an invariable stimulant to the vice of self-abuse, onanism, masturbation, call it what you will. In young or old, man or woman, boy or girl, modern pornography is a direct provocative of masturbation. It cannot be otherwise. When the grey ones wail that the young man and the young woman went and had sexual intercourse, they are bewailing the fact that the young man and the young woman didn't go separately and masturbate. Sex must go somewhere, especially in young people. So, in our glorious civilization, it goes in masturbation. And the mass of our popular literature, the bulk of our popular amusements just exists to provoke masturbation. Masturbation is the one thoroughly secret act of the human being, more secret even than excrementation. It is the one functional result of sex-secrecy, and it is stimulated and provoked by our glorious popular literature of pretty pornography, which rubs on the dirty secret without letting you know what is happening.

Now I have heard men, teachers and clergymen, commend masturbation as the solution of an otherwise insoluble sex problem. This at least is honest. The sex problem is there, and you can't just will it away. There it is, and under the ban of secrecy and taboo in mother and father, teacher, friend and foe, it has found its own solution, the solution of masturbation.

But what about the solution? Do we accept it? Do all the grey ones of this world accept it? If so, they must now accept it openly. We can none of us pretend any longer to be blind to the fact of masturbation, in young and old, man and woman. The moral guardians who are prepared to censor all open and plain portrayal of sex must now be made to give their only justification: We prefer that the people shall masturbate. If this preference is open and declared, then the existing forms of censorship are justified. If the moral guardians prefer that the people shall masturbate, then their present behaviour is correct, and popular amusements are as they should be. If sexual intercourse is deadly sin, and masturbation is comparatively pure and harmless, then all is well. Let things continue as they now are.

Is masturbation so harmless, though? Is it even comparatively pure and harmless? Not to my thinking. In the young, a certain amount of masturbation is inevitable, but not therefore natural. I think, there is no boy or girl who masturbates without feeling a sense of shame, anger and futility. Following the excitement comes the shame, anger, humiliation and the sense of futility. This sense of futility and humiliation deepens as the years go on, into a suppressed rage, because of the impossibility of escape. The one thing that it seems impossible to escape from, once the habit is formed, is masturbation. It goes on and on, on into old age, in spite of marriage or love affairs or anything else. And it always carries this secret feeling of futility

C 33

and humiliation, futility and humiliation. And this is, perhaps, the deepest and most dangerous cancer of our civilization. Instead of being a comparatively pure and harmless vice, masturbation is certainly the most dangerous sexual vice that a society can be afflicted with, in the long run. Comparatively pure it may be—purity being what it is. But harmless! ! !

The great danger of masturbation lies in its merely exhaustive nature. In sexual intercourse, there is a give and take. A new stimulus enters as the native stimulus departs. Something quite new is added as the old surcharge is removed. And this is so in all sexual intercourse where two creatures are concerned, even in the homosexual intercourse. But in masturbation there is nothing but loss. There is no reciprocity. There is merely the spending away of a certain force, and no return. The body remains, in a sense, a corpse, after the act of self-abuse. There is no change, only deadening. There is what we call dead loss. And this is not the case in any act of sexual intercourse between two people. Two people may destroy one another in

34

sex. But they cannot just produce the null effect of masturbation.

The only positive effect of masturbation is that it seems to release a certain mental energy, in some people. But it is mental energy which manifests itself always in the same way, in a vicious circle of analysis and impotent criticism, or else a vicious circle of false and easy sympathy, sentimentalities. The sentimentalism and the niggling analysis, often self-analysis, of most of our modern literature is a sign of self-abuse. It is the manifestation of masturbation, the sort of conscious activity stimulated by masturbation, whether male or female. The outstanding feature of such consciousness is that there is no real object, there is only subject. This is just the same whether it be a novel or a work of science. The author never escapes from himself, he pads along within the vicious circle of himself. There is hardly a writer living who gets out of the vicious circle of himself—or a painter either. Hence the lack of creation, and the stupendous amount of production. It is a masturbation result, within the vicious circle of the self. It is self-absorption made public.

And of course the process is exhaustive. The real masturbation of Englishmen began only in the nineteenth century. It has continued with an increasing emptying of the real vitality and the real *being* of men, till now people are little more than shells of people. Most of the responses are dead, most of the awareness is dead, nearly all the constructive activity is dead, and all that remains is a sort of shell, a half-empty creature fatally self-preoccupied and incapable of either giving or taking. Incapable either of giving or taking, in the vital self. And this is masturbation result. Enclosed within the vicious circle of the self, with no vital contacts outside, the self becomes emptier and emptier, till it is almost a nullus, a nothingness.

But null or nothing as it may be, it still hangs on to the dirty little secret, which it must still secretly rub and inflame. Forever the vicious circle. And it has a weird, blind will of its own.

One of my most sympathetic critics wrote: 'If Mr. Lawrence's attitude to sex were adopted, then two things would disappear, the love lyric and the smoking-room story.' And this, I think, is true. But it depends on which love-lyric he means. If it is the: *Who is Sylvia, what is she?*—then it may just as well disappear. All that pure and noble and heaven-blessed stuff is only the counterpart to the smoking-room story. *Du bist wie eine Blume!* Jawohl! One can see the elderly gentleman laying his hands on the head of the pure maiden and praying God to keep her forever so pure, so clean and beautiful. Very nice for him! Just pornography! tickling the dirty little secret and rolling his eyes to heaven! He knows perfectly well that if God keeps the maiden so clean and pure and beautiful—in his vulgar sense of clean and pure—for a few more years, then she'll be an unhappy old maid, and not pure nor beautiful at all, only stale and pathetic. Sentimentality is a sure sign of pornography. Why should 'sadness strike through the heart' of the old gentleman, because the maid was pure and beautiful? Anybody but a masturbator would have been glad and would have thought: What a lovely bride for some lucky man!—But no, not the self-enclosed, pornographic masturbator.

Sadness has to strike into his beastly heart!—Away with such love-lyrics, we've had too much of their pornographic poison, tickling the dirty little secret and rolling the eyes to heaven.

But if it is a question of the sound love-lyric, '*My love is like a red, red rose——!*' then we are on other ground. My love is like a red, red rose only when she's *not* like a pure, pure lily. And nowadays the pure, pure lilies are mostly festering, anyhow. Away with them and their lyrics. Away with the pure, pure lily lyric, along with the smoking-room story. They are counterparts, and the one is as pornographic as the other. *Du bist wie eine Blume*— is really as pornographic as a dirty story: tickling the dirty little secret and rolling the eyes to heaven. But oh, if only Robert Burns had been accepted for what he is, then love might still have been like a red, red rose.

The vicious circle, the vicious circle! The vicious circle of masturbation! The vicious circle of self-consciousness that is never *fully* self-conscious, never fully and openly conscious, but always harping on the dirty little secret. The vicious circle of secrecy, in parents, teachers, friends—everybody. The specially vicious circle of family. The vast conspiracy of secrecy in the press, and at the same time the endless tickling of the dirty little secret. The endless masturbation! and the endless purity! The vicious circle!

How to get out of it? There is only one way: Away with the secret! No more secrecy! The only way to stop the terrible mental itch about sex is to come out quite simply and naturally into the open with it. It is terribly difficult, for the secret is cunning as a crab. Yet the thing to do is to make a beginning. The man who said to his exasperating daughter: 'My child, the only pleasure I ever had out of you was the pleasure I had in begetting you' —has already done a great deal to release both himself and her from the dirty little secret.

How to get out of the dirty little secret! It is, as a matter of fact, extremely difficult for us secretive moderns. You can't do it by being wise and scientific about it, like Dr. Marie Stopes: though to be wise and scientific like Dr. Marie Stopes is better than to be utterly hypocritical, like the grey ones.

But by being wise and scientific in the serious and earnest manner you only tend to disinfect the dirty little secret, and either kill sex altogether with too much seriousness and intellect, or else leave it a miserable disinfected secret. The unhappy 'free and pure' love of so many people who have taken out the dirty little secret and thoroughly disinfected it with scientific words is apt to be more pathetic even than the common run of dirty-little-secret love. The danger is, that in killing the dirty little secret, you kill dynamic sex altogether, and leave only the scientific and deliberate mechanism.

This is what happens to many of those who become seriously 'free' in their sex, free and pure. They have mentalized sex till it is nothing at all, nothing at all but a mental quantity. And the final result is disaster, every time.

The same is true, in an even greater proportion, of the emancipated bohemians: and very many of the young are bohemian to-day, whether they ever set foot in bohemia or not. But the bohemian is 'sex free'. The dirty little secret is no secret either to him or her. It is, indeed, a most blatantly open question. There is nothing they don't say: everything that can be revealed is revealed. And they do as they wish.

And then what? They have apparently killed the dirty little secret, but somehow, they have killed everything else too. Some of the dirt still sticks perhaps; sex remains still dirty. But the thrill of secrecy is gone. Hence the terrible dreariness and depression of modern Bohemia, and the inward dreariness and emptiness of so many young people of to-day. They have killed, they imagine, the dirty little secret. The thrill of secrecy is gone. Some of the dirt remains. And for the rest, depression, inertia, lack of life. For sex is the fountain-head of our energetic life, and now the fountain ceases to flow.

Why? For two reasons. The idealists along the Marie Stopes line, and the young bohemians of to-day have killed the dirty little secret as far as their personal self goes. But they are still under its dominion socially. In the social world, in the press, in literature, film, theatre, wireless, everywhere purity and the dirty little secret reigns supreme.

At home, at the dinner table, it is just the same. It is the same wherever you go. The young girl, and the young woman is by tacit assumption pure, virgin, sexless. *Du bist wie eine Blume*. She, poor thing, knows quite well that flowers, even lilies, have tippling yellow anthers and a sticky stigma, sex, rolling sex. But to the popular mind flowers are sexless things, and when a girl is told she is like a flower, it means she is sexless and ought to be sexless. She herself knows quite well she isn't sexless and she isn't merely like a flower. But how bear up against the great social lie forced on her? She can't! She succumbs, and the dirty little secret triumphs. She loses her interest in sex, as far as men are concerned, but the vicious circle of masturbation and self-consciousness encloses her even still faster.

This is one of the disasters of young life to-day. Personally, and among themselves, a great many, perhaps a majority of the young people of to-day, have come out into the open with sex and laid salt on the tail of the dirty little secret. And this is a very good thing. But in public, in the social world, the young are still entirely under the shadow of the grey elderly ones. The grey elderly ones belong to the last century, the eunuch century, the century of the mealy-mouthed lie, the century that has tried to destroy humanity, the nineteenth century. All our grey ones are left over from this century. And they rule us. They rule us with the grey, mealy-mouthed, canting lie of that great century of lies which, thank God, we are drifting away from. But they rule us still with the lie, for the lie, in the name of the lie. And they are too heavy and too numerous, the grey ones. It doesn't matter what government it is. They are all grey ones, left over from the last century, the century of mealy-mouthed liars, the century of purity and the dirty little secret.

So there is one cause for the depression of the young; the public reign of the mealy-mouthed lie, purity and the dirty little secret, which they themselves have privately overthrown. Having killed a good deal of the lie in their own private lives, the young are still enclosed and imprisoned within the great public lie of the grey ones. Hence the excess, the extravagance, the hysteria, and then the weakness, the feebleness, the pathetic silliness of the modern youth. They are all in a sort of prison, the prison of a great lie and a society of elderly liars. And this is one of the reasons, perhaps the main reason why the sex-flow is dying out of the young, the real energy is dying away. They are enclosed within a lie, and the sex won't flow. For the length of a complete lie is never more than three generations, and the young are the fourth generation of the nineteenth-century lie.

The second reason why the sex-flow is dying is of course, that the young, in spite of their emancipation, are still enclosed within the vicious circle of self-conscious masturbation. They are thrown back into it, when they try to escape, by the enclosure of the vast public lie of purity and the dirty little secret. The most emancipated bohemians, who swank most about sex, are still utterly self-conscious and enclosed within the narcissus-masturbation circle. They have perhaps less sex even than the grey ones. The whole thing has been driven up into their heads. There isn't even the

44

lurking hole of a dirty little secret. Their sex is more mental than their arithmetic; and as vital physical creatures they are more non-existent than ghosts. The modern bohemian is indeed a kind of ghost, not even narcissus, only the image of narcissus reflected on the face of the audience. The dirty little secret is most difficult to kill. You may put it to death publicly a thousand times, and still it reappears, like a crab, stealthily from under the submerged rocks of the personality. The French, who are supposed to be so open about sex, will perhaps be the last to kill the dirty little secret. Perhaps they don't want to. Anyhow mere publicity won't do it.

You may parade sex abroad, but you will not kill the dirty little secret. You may read all the novels of Marcel Proust, with everything there in all detail. Yet you will not kill the dirty little secret. You will perhaps only make it more cunning. You may even bring about a state of utter indifference and sex-inertia, still without killing the dirty little secret. Or you may be the most wispy and enamoured little Don Juan of modern days, and still the core of your spirit merely be the dirty little secret. That is to say, you will still be in the narcissus-masturbation circle, the vicious circle of self-enclosure. For whenever the dirty little secret exists, it exists as the centre of the vicious circle of masturbation self-enclosure. And whenever you have the vicious circle of masturbation self-enclosure, you have at the core the dirty little secret. And the most high-flown sex-emancipated young people to-day are perhaps the most fatally and nervously enclosed within the masturbation self-enclosure. Nor do they want to get out of it, for there would be nothing left to come out.

But some people surely do want to come out of the awful self-enclosure. To-day, practically everybody is self-conscious and imprisoned in self-consciousness. It is the joyful result of the dirty little secret. Vast numbers of people don't want to come out of the prison of their self-consciousness: they have so little left to come out with. But some people, surely, want to escape this doom of self-enclosure which is the doom of our civilization. There is surely a proud minority that wants once and for all to be free of the dirty little secret.

And the way to do it is, first, to fight the sentimental lie of purity and the dirty little secret wherever you meet it, inside yourself or in the world outside. Fight the great lie of the nineteenth century, which has soaked through our sex and our bones. It means fighting with almost every breath, for the lie is ubiquitous.

Then secondly, in his adventure of self-consciousness a man must come to the limits of himself and become aware of something beyond him. A man must be self-conscious enough to know his own limits, and to be aware of that which surpasses him. What surpasses me is the very urge of life that is within me, and this life urges me to forget myself and to yield to the stirring half-born impulse to smash up the vast lie of the world, and make a new world. If my life is merely to go on in a vicious circle of self-enclosure, masturbating self-consciousness, it is worth nothing to me. If my individual life is to be enclosed within the huge corrupt lie of society to-day, purity and the dirty little secret, then it is worth not much to me.

Freedom is a very great reality. But it means, above all things, freedom from lies. It is first, freedom from myself, from the lie of myself, from the lie of my all-importance, even to myself; it is freedom from the self-conscious masturbating thing I am, self-enclosed. And second, freedom from the vast lie of the social world, the lie of purity and the dirty little secret. All the other monstrous lies lurk under the cloak of this one primary lie. The monstrous lie of money lurks under the cloak of purity. Kill the purity-lie, and the money-lie will be defenceless.

We have to be sufficiently conscious, and self-conscious, to know our own limits and to be aware of the greater urge within us and beyond us. Then we cease to be primarily interested in ourselves. Then we learn to leave ourselves alone, in all the affective centres: not to force our feelings in any way, and never to force our sex. Then we make the great onslaught on to the outside lie, the inside lie being settled. And that is freedom and the fight for freedom.

The greatest of all lies in the modern world is the

lie of purity and the dirty little secret. The grey ones left over from the nineteenth century are the embodiment of this lie. They dominate in society, in the press, in literature, everywhere. And, naturally, they lead the vast mob of the general public along with them.

Which means, of course, perpetual censorship of anything that would militate against the lie of purity and the dirty little secret, and perpetual encouragement of what may be called permissible pornography, pure, but tickling the dirty little secret under the delicate underclothing. The grey ones will pass and will commend floods of evasive pornography, and will suppress every outspoken word.

The law is a mere figment. In his article on the 'Censorship of Books', in the *Nineteenth Century*, Viscount Brentford, the late Home Secretary, says: 'Let it be remembered that the publishing of an obscene book, the issue of an obscene post-card or pornographic photograph—are all offences against the law of the land, and the Secretary of State who is the general authority for the maintenance of law and order most clearly and definitely cannot discriminate between one offence and another in discharge of his duty.'

So he winds up, *ex cathedra* and infallible. But only ten lines above he has written: 'I agree, that if the law were pushed to its logical conclusion, the printing and publication of such books as *The Decameron*, Benvenuto Cellini's *Life*, and Burton's *Arabian Nights* might form the subject of proceedings. But the ultimate sanction of all law is public opinion, and I do not believe for one moment that prosecution in respect of books that have been in circulation for many centuries would command public support.'

Ooray then for public opinion! It only needs that a few more years shall roll. But now we see that the Secretary of State most clearly and definitely *does* discriminate between one offence and another in discharge of his duty. Simple and admitted discrimination on his part! Yet what is this public opinion? Just more lies on the part of the grey ones. They would suppress Benvenuto tomorrow, if they dared. But they would make laughing-stocks of themselves, because *tradition* backs up Benvenuto. It isn't public opinion at all. It is the grey ones afraid of making still bigger fools of themselves. But the case is simple. If the grey ones are going to be backed by a general public, then every new book that would smash the mealy-mouthed lie of the nineteenth century will be suppressed as it appears. Yet let the grey ones beware. The general public is nowadays a very unstable affair, and no longer loves its grey ones so dearly, with their old lie. And there is another public, the small public of the minority, which hates the lie and the grey ones that perpetuate the lie, and which has its own dynamic ideas about pornography and obscenity. You can't fool all the people all the time, even with purity and a dirty little secret.

And this minority public knows well that the books of many contemporary writers, both big and lesser fry, are far more pornographical than the liveliest story in *The Decameron*: because they tickle the dirty little secret and excite to private masturbation, which the wholesome Boccaccio never does. And the minority public knows full well that the most obscene painting on a Greek vase—*Thou still unravished bride of quietness*—is not as pornographical as the close-up kisses on the film, which excite men and women to secret and separate masturbation.

And perhaps one day even the general public will desire to look the thing in the face, and see for itself the difference between the sneaking masturbation pornography of the press, the film, and present-day popular literature, and then the creative portrayals of the sexual impulse that we have in Boccaccio or the Greek vase-paintings or some Pompeian art, and which are necessary for the fulfilment of our consciousness.

As it is, the public mind is to-day bewildered on this point, bewildered almost to idiocy. When the police raided my picture show, they did not in the least know what to take. So they took every picture where the smallest bit of the sex organ of either man or woman showed. Quite regardless of subject or meaning or anything else: they would allow anything, these dainty policemen in a picture show, except the actual sight of a fragment of the human *pudenda*. This was the police test. The dabbing on of a postage stamp—especially a green one that could be called a leaf—would in most cases have been quite sufficient to satisfy this 'public opinion'.

It is, we can only repeat, a condition of idiocy. And if the purity-with-a-dirty-little-secret lie is kept up much longer, the mass of society will really be an idiot, and a dangerous idiot at that. For the public is made up of individuals. And each individual has sex, and is pivoted on sex. And if, with purity and dirty little secrets you drive every individual into the masturbation self-enclosure, and keep him there, then you will produce a state of general idiocy. For the masturbation self-enclosure produces idiots. Perhaps if we are all idiots, we shan't know it. But God preserve us.

INTRODUCTION TO PAINTING

INTRODUCTION TO PAINTING

The reason the English produce so few painters is not that they are, as a nation, devoid of a genuine feeling for visual art: though, to look at their productions, and to look at the mess which has been made of actual English landscape, one might really conclude that they were, and leave it at that. But it is not the fault of the God that made them. They are made with æsthetic sensibilities the same as anybody else. The fault lies in the English attitude to life.

The English, and the Americans following them, are paralysed by fear. That is what thwarts and distorts the Anglo-Saxon existence, this paralysis of fear. It thwarts life, it distorts vision, and it strangles impulse: this overmastering fear. And fear what of, in heaven's name? What is the Anglo-Saxon stock to-day so petrified with fear about? We have to answer that before we can understand the English failure in the visual arts: for on the whole, it is a failure.

It is an old fear, which seemed to dig into the English soul at the time of the Renaissance. Nothing could be more lovely and fearless than Chaucer. But already Shakespeare is morbid with fear, fear of consequences. That is the strange phenomenon of the English Renaissance: this mystic terror of the consequences, the consequences of action. Italy too had her reaction, at the end of the sixteenth century, and showed a similar fear. But not so profound, so overmastering. Aretino was anything but timorous: he was bold as any Renaissance novelist, and went one better.

What appeared to take full grip on the northern consciousness at the end of the sixteenth century was a terror, almost a horror of sexual life. The Elizabethans, grand as we think them, started it.

The real 'mortal coil' in Hamlet is all sexual, the young man's horror of his mother's incest, sex carrying with it a wild and nameless terror which, it seems to me, it had never carried before. Œdipus and Hamlet are very different in this respect. In Œdipus there is no recoil in horror from sex itself. Greek drama never shows us that. The horror, when it is present in Greek tragedy, is against *destiny*, man caught in the toils of destiny. But with the Renaissance itself, particularly in England, the horror is sexual. Orestes is dogged by destiny and driven mad by the Eumenides. But Hamlet is overpowered by horrible revulsion from his physical connection with his mother, which makes him recoil in similar revulsion from Ophelia, and almost from his father, even as a ghost. He is horrified at the merest suggestion of physical connection, as if it were an unspeakable taint.

This no doubt is all in the course of the growth of the 'spiritual-mental' consciousness, at the expense of the instinctive intuitive consciousness. Man came to have his own body in horror, especially in its sexual implications: and so he began to suppress with all his might his instinctive-intuitive consciousness, which is so radical, so physical, so sexual. Cavalier poetry, love poetry, is already devoid of body. Donne, after the exacerbated revulsion-attraction excitement of his earlier poetry, becomes a divine. 'Drink to me only with thine eyes,' sings the cavalier: an expression incredible in Chaucer's poetry. 'I could not love thee, dear, so much, loved I not honour more,' sings the cavalier lover. In Chaucer the 'dear' and the 'honour' would have been more or less identical.

But with the Elizabethans the grand rupture had started, in the human consciousness, the mental consciousness recoiling in violence away from the physical, instinctive-intuitive. To the Restoration dramatists sex is, on the whole, a dirty business, but they more or less glory in the dirt. Fielding tries in vain to defend the Old Adam. Richardson with his calico purity and his underclothing excitements sweeps all before him. Swift goes mad with sex and excrement revulsion. Sterne flings a bit of the same excrement humorously around. And physical consciousness gives a last song in

Burns, then is dead. Wordsworth, Keats, Shelley, the Brontës, all are post-mortem poets. The essential instinctive-intuitive body is dead, and worshipped in death—all very unhealthy. Till Swinburne and Oscar Wilde try to start a revival from the mental field. Swinburne's 'white thighs' are purely mental.

Now in England—and following, in America—the physical self was not just fig-leafed over or suppressed in public, as was the case in Italy and on most of the Continent. In England it excited a strange horror and terror. And this extra morbidity came, I believe, from the great shock of syphilis and the realization of the consequences of the disease. Wherever syphilis, or 'pox', came from, it was fairly new in England at the end of the fifteenth century. But by the end of the sixteenth, its ravages were obvious, and the shock of them had just penetrated the thoughtful and the imaginative consciousness. The royal families of England and Scotland were syphilitic, Edward VI and Elizabeth born with the inherited consequences of the disease. Edward VI died of it, while still a boy. Mary died childless and in utter depression. Elizabeth had no eyebrows, her teeth went rotten, she must have felt herself, somewhere, utterly unfit for marriage, poor thing. That was the grisly horror that lay behind the glory of Queen Bess. And so the Tudors died out: and another syphilitic-born unfortunate came to the throne, in the person of James I. Mary Queen of Scots had no more luck than the Tudors, apparently. Apparently Darnley was reeking with the pox, though probably at first she did not know it. But when the Archbishop of St. Andrew's was christening her baby James, afterwards James I of England, the old clergyman was so dripping with pox that she was terrified lest he should give it to the infant. And she need not have troubled, for the wretched infant had brought it into the world with him, from that fool Darnley. So James I of England slobbered and shambled, and was the wisest fool in Christendom, and the Stuarts likewise died out, the stock enfeebled by the disease.

With the Royal families of England and Scotland in this condition, we can judge what the noble houses, the nobility of both nations, given to free living and promiscuous pleasure, must have been like. England traded with the East and with America; England, unknowing, had opened her doors to the disease. The English aristocracy travelled and had curious taste in loves. And pox entered the blood of the nation, particularly of the upper classes, who had more chance of infection. And after it had entered the blood, it entered the consciousness, and it hit the vital imagination.

It is possible that the effects of syphilis and the conscious realization of its consequences gave a great blow to the Spanish psyche, precisely at this period. And it is possible that Italian society, which was on the whole so untravelled, had no connection with America, and was so privately self-contained, suffered less from the disease. Some-one ought to make a thorough study of the effects of 'pox' on the minds and the emotions and imagination of the various nations of Europe, at about the time of our Elizabethans.

The apparent effect on the Elizabethans and the Restoration wits is curious. They appear to take the whole thing as a joke. The common oath, 'Pox on you!' was almost funny. But how common the oath was! How the word 'pox' was in every mind, and in every mouth. It is one of the words that haunt Elizabethan speech. Taken very manly, with a great deal of Falstaffian bluff, treated as a huge joke! Pox! Why, he's got the pox! Ha-ha! What's he been after?

There is just the same attitude among the common run of men to-day with regard to the minor sexual diseases. Syphilis is no longer regarded as a joke, according to my experience. The very word itself frightens men. You could joke with the word 'pox'. You can't joke with the word 'syphilis'. The change of word has killed the joke. But men still joke about *clap*! which is a minor sexual disease. They pretend to think it manly, even, to have the disease, or to have had it. 'What! Never had a shot of clap!' cries one gentleman to another. 'Why, where have you been all your life!' If we changed the word and insisted on 'gonorrhœa', or whatever it is, in place of 'clap', the joke would die. And anyhow I have had young men come to me green

64

and quaking, afraid they've caught 'a shot of clap'.

Now, in spite of all the Elizabethan jokes about pox, pox was no joke to them. A joke may be a very brave way of meeting a calamity, or it may be a very cowardly way. Myself, I consider the Elizabethan pox joke a purely cowardly attitude. They didn't think it funny, for by God it *wasn't* funny. Even poor Elizabeth's lack of eyebrows and her rotten teeth were not funny. And they all knew it. They may not have known it was the direct result of pox: though probably they did. This fact remains, that no man can contract syphilis, or any deadly sexual disease, without feeling the most shattering and profound terror go through him, through the very roots of his being. And no man can look without a sort of horror on the effects of a sexual disease in another person. We are so constituted that we are all at once horrified and terrified. The fear and dread has been so great, that the pox joke was invented as an evasion, and following that, the great hush! hush! was imposed. Man was *too* frightened, that's the top and bottom of it.

But now, with remedies discovered, we need no longer be *too* frightened. We can begin, after all these years, to face the matter. After the most fearful damage has been done.

For an overmastering fear is poison to the human psyche. And this overmastering fear, like some horrible secret tumour, has been poisoning our consciousness ever since the Elizabethans, who first woke up witn dread to the entry of the original syphilitic poison into the blood.

I know nothing about medicine and very little about diseases, and my facts are such as I have picked up in casual reading. Nevertheless I am convinced that the secret awareness of syphilis, and the utter secret terror and horror of it, has had an enormous and incalculable effect on the English consciousness, and on the American. Even when the fear has never been formulated, there it has lain, potent and overmastering. I am convinced that *some* of Shakespeare's horror and despair, in his tragedies, arose from the shock of his consciousness of syphilis. I don't suggest for one moment Shakespeare ever contracted syphilis. I have never

66

had syphilis myself. Yet I know and confess how profound is my fear of the disease, and more than fear, my horror. In fact, I don't think I am so very much afraid of it. I am more horrified, inwardly and deeply, at the idea of its existence.

All this sounds very far from the art of painting. But it is not so far as it sounds. The appearance of syphilis in our midst gave a fearful blow to our sexual life. The real natural innocence of Chaucer was impossible after that. The very sexual act of procreation might bring as one of its consequences a foul disease, and the unborn might be tainted from the moment of conception. Fearful thought! It is truly a fearful thought, and all the centuries of getting used to it won't help us. It remains a fearful thought, and to free ourselves from this fearful dread we should use all our wits and all our efforts, not stick our heads in the sand of some idiotic joke or still more idiotic don't-mention-it. The fearful thought of the consequences of syphilis, or of any sexual disease, upon the unborn gives a shock to the impetus of fatherhood in any man, even the cleanest. Our consciousness is a strange thing, and the knowledge of a certain fact may wound it mortally, even if the fact does not touch us directly. And so I am certain that *some* of Shakespeare's father-murder complex, *some* of Hamlet's horror of his mother, of his uncle, of all old men, came from the feeling that fathers may transmit syphilis, or syphilis-consequences, to children. I don't know even whether Shakespeare was actually aware of the consequences to a child born of a syphilitic father or mother. He may not have been, though most probably he was. But he certainly was aware of the effects of syphilis itself, especially on men. And this awareness struck at his deep sex imagination, at his instinct for fatherhood, and brought in an element of terror and abhorrence there where man should feel anything but terror and abhorrence, into the procreative act.

The terror-horror element which had entered the imagination with regard to the sexual and procreative act was at least partly responsible for the rise of Puritanism, the beheading of the king-father Charles, and the establishment of the New

England colonies. If America really sent us syphilis, she got back the full recoil of the horror of it, in her Puritanism.

But deeper even than this, the terror-horror element led to the crippling of the consciousness of man. Very elementary in man is his sexual and procreative being, and on his sexual and procreative being depend many of his deepest instincts and the flow of his intuition. A deep instinct of kinship joins men together, and the kinship of flesh-and-blood keeps the warm flow of intuitional awareness streaming between human beings. Our true awareness of one another is intuitional, not mental. Attraction between people is really instinctive and intuitional, not an affair of judgment. And in mutual attraction lies perhaps the deepest pleasure in life, mutual attraction which may make us 'like' our travelling companion for the two or three hours we are together, then no more, or mutual attraction that may deepen to powerful love, and last a lifetime.

The terror-horror element struck a blow at our feeling of physical communion. In fact it almost killed it. We have become ideal beings, creatures that exist in idea, to one another, rather than flesh-and-blood kin. And with the collapse of the feeling of physical, flesh-and-blood oneness, and the substitution of an ideal, social or political oneness, came the failing of our intuitive awareness, and the great unease, the *nervousness* of mankind. We are *afraid* of the instincts. We are *afraid* of the intuition within us. We suppress the instincts, and we cut off our intuitional awareness from one another and from the world. The reason being some great shock to the procreative self. Now we know one another only as ideal or social or political entities, fleshless, bloodless, and cold, like Bernard Shaw's creatures. Intuitively we are dead to one another, we have all gone cold.

But by intuition alone can man *really* be aware of man, or of the living, substantial world. By intuition alone can man love and know either woman or world, and by intuition alone can he bring forth again images of magic awareness which we call art. In the past men brought forth images of magic awareness, and now it is the convention to admire these images. The convention says, for example, we must admire Botticelli or Giorgione, so Baedeker stars the pictures, and we admire them. But it is all a fake. Even those that get a thrill, even when they call it ecstasy, from these old pictures, are only undergoing a cerebral excitation. Their deeper responses, down in the intuitive and instinctive body, are not touched. They cannot be, because they are dead. A dead intuitive body stands there and gazes at the corpse of beauty: and usually it is completely and honestly bored; sometimes it feels a mental coruscation which it calls an ecstasy or an æsthetic response.

Modern people, but particularly English and Americans, *cannot* feel anything with the whole imagination. They can see the living body of imagery as little as a blind man can see colour. The imaginative vision, which includes physical intuitional perception, they *have not got*. Poor things, it is dead in them. And they stand in front of a Botticelli Venus, which they know is conventionally 'beautiful', much as a blind man might stand in front of a bunch of roses and pinks and monkey-mush, saying: 'Oh, do tell me which is red, let me feel red! Now let me feel white! Oh, let me feel it! What is this I am feeling? Monkey-mush? Is it white? Oh, do you say it is yellow blotched with orange-brown? Oh, but I can't feel it! What *can* it be? Is white velvety, or just silky?'

So the poor blind man! Yet he may have an acute perception of alive beauty. Merely by touch and scent, his intuitions being alive, the blind man may have a genuine and soul-satisfying experience of imagery. But not pictorial images. These are forever beyond him.

So those poor English and Americans in front of the Botticelli Venus. They stare so hard, they do so *want* to see. And their eyesight is perfect. But all they can see is a sort of nude woman on a sort of shell on a sort of pretty greenish water. As a rule they rather dislike the 'unnaturalness' or 'affectation' of it. If they are highbrows they may get little self-conscious thrills of æsthetic excitement. But real imaginative awareness, which is so largely physical, is denied them. *Ils n'ont pas de quoi,* as the Frenchman said of the angels, when asked if they made love in heaven.

Ah, the dear highbrows who gaze in a sort of ecstasy and get a correct mental thrill! Their poor highbrow bodies stand there as dead as dustbins, and can no more feel the sway of complete imagery upon them than they can feel any other real sway. *Ils n'ont pas de quoi.* The instincts and the intuitions are so nearly dead in them and they fear even the feeble remains. Their fear of the instincts and intuitions is even greater than that of the English Tommy who calls: 'Eh, Jack! Come an' look at this girl standin' wi' no clothes on, an' two blokes spittin' at 'er'. That is his vision of Botticelli's Venus. It is, for him, complete, for he is void of image-seeing imagination. But at least he doesn't have to work up a cerebral excitation, as the highbrow does, who is really just as void.

All alike, cultured and uncultured, they are still dominated by that unnamed, yet overmastering dread and hate of the instincts deep in the body, dread of the strange intuitional awareness of the body, dread of anything but ideas, which *can't* contain bacteria. And the dread all works back to a dread of the procreative body, and is partly traceable to the shock of the awareness of syphilis.

The dread of the instincts included the dread of intuitional awareness. 'Beauty is a snare'—'Beauty is but skin-deep'—'Handsome is as handsome does' —'Looks don't count'—'Don't judge by appearances'—if we only realized it, there are thousands of these vile proverbs which have been dinned into us for over two hundred years. They are all of them false. Beauty is not a snare, nor is it skin-deep, since it always involves a certain loveliness of modelling, and handsome doers are often ugly and objectionable people, and if you ignore the look of the thing you plaster England with slums and produce at last a state of spiritual depression that is suicidal, and if you don't judge by appearances, that is, if you can't trust the *impression* which things make on you, you are a fool. But all these base-born proverbs, born in the cash-box, hit direct against the intuitional consciousness. Naturally, man gets a great deal of his life's satisfaction from beauty, from a certain sensuous pleasure in the look of the thing. The old Englishman built his hut of a cottage with a childish joy in its appearance, purely intuitional and direct. The modern Englishman has a few borrowed ideas, simply doesn't know *what* to feel, and makes a silly mess of it. The intuitional faculty, which alone relates us in direct awareness to physical things and substantial presences, is atrophied and dead, and we don't know *what* to feel. We know we ought to feel something, but what?—oh, tell us what! And this is true of all nations, the French and Italians as much as the English. Look at new French suburbs! Go through the crockery and furniture departments in the *Dames de France* or any big shop. The blood in the body stands still, before such *crétin* ugliness. One has to decide that the modern bourgeois is a *crétin*.

This movement against the instincts and the intuition took on a moral tone in all countries. It started in hatred. Let us never forget that modern morality has its roots in hatred, a deep, evil hate of the instinctive, intuitional, procreative body. This hatred is made more virulent by fear, and an extra poison is added to the fear by unconscious horror of syphilis. And so we come to modern bourgeois consciousness, which turns upon the secret pole of fear and hate. That is the real pivot of all bourgeois consciousness in all countries: fear and hate of the instinctive, intuitional, procreative body in man or woman. But of course this fear and hate had to take on a righteous appearance, so it became moral, said that the instincts, intuitions and all the activities of the procreative body were evil, and promised a *reward* for their suppression. That is the great clue to bourgeois psychology: the reward business. It is screamingly obvious in Maria Edgeworth's tales, which must have done unspeakable damage to ordinary people—Be good and you'll have money. Be wicked, and you'll be utterly penniless at last, and the good ones will have to offer you a little charity. This is sound working morality in the world. And it makes one realize that, even to Milton, the true hero of *Paradise Lost* must be Satan. But by this baited morality the masses were caught and enslaved to industrialism before ever they knew it; the good ones got hold of the goods, and our modern 'civilization' of money, machines and wage-slaves was inaugurated. The very pivot of it, let us never forget, being fear and hate, the most intimate fear and hate, fear and hate of one's own instinctive, intuitive body, and fear and hate of every other man's and every other woman's warm, procreative body and imagination.

Now it is obvious what result this will leave on the plastic arts, which depend entirely on the representation of substantial bodies, and on the intuitional perception of the *reality* of substantial bodies. The reality of substantial bodies can only be preserved by the imagination, and the imagination is a kindled state of consciousness in which intuitive awareness predominates. The plastic arts are all imagery, and imagery is the body of our imaginative life, and our imaginative life is a great joy and fulfilment to us, for the imagination is a more powerful and more comprehensive flow of consciousness than our ordinary flow. In the flow of true imagination we know in full, mentally and physically at once, in a greater, enkindled awareness. At the maximum of our imagination we are religious. And if we deny our imagination, and have no imaginative life, we are poor worms who have never lived.

In the seventeenth and eighteenth centuries we have the deliberate denial of intuitive awareness, and we see the results on the arts. Vision became more optical, less intuitive, and painting began to flourish. But what painting! Watteau, Ingres, Poussin, Chardin have some imaginative glow still. They are still somewhat free. The puritan and the intellectual has not yet struck them down with his fear and hate obsessions. But look at England! Hogarth, Reynolds, Gainsborough, they all are already bourgeois. The coat is really more important than the man. It is amazing how important clothes suddenly become, how they *cover* the subject. An old Reynolds colonel in a red uniform is much more a uniform than an individual, and as for Gainsborough, all you can say is: What a lovely dress and hat! What really expensive Italian silk! This painting of garments continued in vogue, till pictures like Sargent's seem to be nothing but yards and yards of satin from the most expensive shops, having some pretty head popped over the top. The imagination is quite dead. The optical vision, a sort of flashy coloured photography of the eye, is rampant.

In Titian, in Velasquez, in Rembrandt, the people are there inside their clothes all right, and the clothes are imbued with the life of individual, the gleam of the warm procreative body comes through all the time, even if it be an old, half-blind woman or a weird, ironic little Spanish princess. But modern people are nothing inside their garments, and a head sticks out at the top and hands stick out of the sleeves, and it is a bore. Or, as in Lawrence, or Raeburn, you have something very pretty but almost a mere cliché, with very little instinctive or intuitional perception to it.

After this, and apart from landscape and water-colour, there is strictly no English painting that exists. As far as I am concerned, the pre-Raphael-ites don't exist, Watts doesn't, Sargent doesn't, and none of the moderns.

There is the exception of Blake. Blake is the only

painter of the first order that England has produced. And unfortunately there is so little Blake, and even in that little the symbolism is often artificially imposed. Nevertheless Blake paints with real intuitional awareness and solid instinctive feeling. He dares handle the living, sensuous human body: a thing which no other Englishman has dared to do. Painters of composition pictures in England, of whom perhaps the best is Watts, never quite get below the level of cliché, sentimentalism, and *funk*. Even Watts is a failure: and the others don't bear mention. They illustrate ideas with clichés in paint.

Landscape, however, is different. Here the English exist and hold their own. But, for me, personally, landscape is always waiting for something to occupy it. Landscape seems to be *meant* as a background to an intense vision of life, so to my feeling painted landscape is background with the real subject left out.

Nevertheless, it can be very lovely, especially in water-colour, which is a more bodiless medium, and doesn't aspire to very substantial existence, and is so small that it doesn't try to make a very deep seizure on the consciousness. Water-colour will always be more of a statement than an experience.

And landscape, on the whole, is the same. It doesn't call up the more powerful responses of the human imagination, the sensual, passional responses. Hence it is the favourite modern form of expression in painting. There is no deep conflict. The instinctive and intuitional consciousness is called into play, but lightly, superficially. It is not confronted with any living, procreated body.

Hence the English have delighted in landscape, and have succeeded in it well. It is a form of escape for them, from the actual human body they so hate and fear, and it is an outlet for their perishing æsthetic desires. For more than a century we have produced delicious water-colours, and Wilson, Crome, Constable, Turner are all great landscape painters. Some of Turner's landscape compositions are, to my feeling, the finest that exist. They still satisfy me more even than Van Gogh's or Cézanne's landscapes, which make a more violent assault on the emotions, and repel a little for that reason. Somehow I don't want landscape to make a violent assault on my feelings. Landscape is background with the figures left out or reduced to the minimum, so let it stay back. Van Gogh's surging earth and Cézanne's explosive or rattling planes worry me. Not being profoundly interested in landscape, I prefer it to be rather quiet and unexplosive.

But of course the English delight in landscape is a delight in escape. It is always the same. The northern races are so innerly afraid of their own bodily existence, which they believe fantastically to be an evil thing—you could never find them feel anything but uneasy shame, or an equally shameful gloating, over the fact that a man was having intercourse with his wife, in his house next door—that all they cry for is an escape. And, especially, art must provide that escape.

It is easy in literature. Shelley is pure escape: the body is sublimated into sublime gas. Keats is more difficult—the body can still be *felt* dissolving in waves of successive death—but the death-business is very satisfactory. The novelists have even a better time. You can get some of the lasciviousness of Hetty Sorrell's 'sin', and you can enjoy condemning her to penal servitude for life. You can thrill to Mr. Rochester's *passion*, and you can enjoy having his eyes burnt out. So it is, all the way: the novel of 'passion'!

But in paint it is more difficult. You cannot paint Hetty Sorrell's sin or Mr. Rochester's passion without being really shocking. And you *daren't* be shocking. It was this fact that unsaddled Watts and Millais. Both might have been painters if they hadn't been Victorians. As it is, each of them is a wash-out.

Which is the poor feeble history of art in England, since we can lay no claim to the great Holbein. And art on the Continent, in the last century? It is more interesting, and has a fuller story. An artist *can* only create what he really religiously *feels* is truth, religious truth really *felt*, in the blood and the bones. The English could never think anything connected with the body *religious*—unless it were the eyes. So they painted the social appearance of human beings, and hoped to give them wonderful eyes. But they *could* think landscape religious, since it had no sensual reality. So they felt religious about it and painted it as well as it could be painted, maybe, from their point of view.

And in France? In France it was more or less the same, but with a difference. The French, being more rational, decided that the body had its place, but that it should be rationalized. The Frenchman of to-day has the most reasonable and rationalized body possible. His conception of sex is basically hygienic. A certain amount of copulation is good for you. *Ça fait du bien au corps!* sums up the physical side of a Frenchman's idea of love, marriage, food, sport and all the rest. Well, it is more sane, anyhow, than the Anglo-Saxon terrors. The Frenchman is afraid of syphilis and afraid of the procreative body, but not quite so deeply. He has known for a long time that you can take precautions. And he is not profoundly imaginative.

Therefore he has been able to paint. But his tendency, just like that of all the modern world, has been to get away from the body, while still paying attention to its hygiene, and still not violently quarrelling with it. Puvis de Chavannes is really as sloppy as all the other spiritual sentimentalizers. Renoir is jolly: *Ça fait du bien au corps!* is his attitude to the flesh. If a woman didn't have buttocks and breasts, she wouldn't be paintable, he said, and he was right. *Ça fait du bien au corps*. What do you paint with, Maître?—With my penis, and be damned! Renoir didn't try to get away from the body. But he had to dodge it in some of its aspects, rob it of its natural terrors, its natural demonishness. He is delightful, but a trifle banal. *Ça fait du bien au corps!* Yet how infinitely much better he is than any English equivalent.

Courbet, Daumier, Dégas, they all painted the human body. But Daumier satirized it, Courbet saw it as a toiling thing, Dégas saw it as a wonderful instrument. They all of them deny it its finest qualities, its deepest instincts, its purest intuitions. They prefer, as it were, to industrialize it. They deny it the best imaginative existence.

And the real grand glamour of modern French art, the real outburst of delight came when the body was at last dissolved of its substance, and made part and parcel of the sunlight-and-shadow scheme. Let us say what we will, but the real grand thrill of modern French art was the discovery of light, the discovery of light, and all the subsequent discoveries of the impressionists, and of the post-impressionists, even Cézanne. No matter how Cézanne may have reacted from the impressionists, it was they, with their deliriously joyful discovery of light and 'free' colour, who really opened his eyes. Probably the most joyous moment in the whole history of painting was the moment when the incipient impressionists discovered light, and with it, colour. Ah, then they made the grand, grand escape into freedom, into infinity, into light and delight. They escaped from the tyranny of solidity and the menace of mass-form. They escaped, they escaped from the dark procreative body which so haunts a man, they escaped into the open air, *plein air* and *plein soleil*: light and almost ecstasy.

Like every other human escape, it meant being hauled back later with the tail between the legs.

Back comes the truant, back to the old doom of matter, of corporate existence, of the body sullen and stubborn and obstinately refusing to be transmuted into pure light, pure colour, or pure anything. It is not concerned with purity. Life isn't. Chemistry and mathematics and ideal religion are, but these are only small bits of life, which is itself bodily, and hence neither pure nor impure.

After the grand escape into impressionism and pure light, pure colour, pure bodilessness—for what is the body but a shimmer of lights and colours!—poor art came home truant and sulky, with its tail between its legs. And it is this return which now interests. We know the escape was illusion, illusion, illusion. The cat had to come back. So now we despise the 'light' blighters too much. We haven't a good word for them. Which is nonsense, for they too are wonderful, even if their escape was into *le grand néant*, the great nowhere.

But the cat came back. And it is the homecoming tom that now has our sympathy: Renoir, to a certain extent, but mostly Cézanne, the sublime little grimalkin, who is followed by Matisse and Gauguin and Derain and Vlaminck and Braque and all the host of other defiant and howling cats that have come back, perforce, to form and substance and *thereness*, instead of delicious nowhereness.

Without wishing to labour the point, one cannot help being amused at the dodge by which the Impressionists made the grand escape from the body. They metamorphosed it into a pure assemblage of shifting lights and shadows, all coloured. A web of woven, luminous colour was a man, or a woman—and so they painted her, or him: a web of woven shadows and gleams. Delicious! and quite true as far as it goes. A purely optical, *visual* truth: which paint is supposed to be. And they painted delicious pictures: a little too delicious. They bore us, at the moment. They bore people like the very modern critics intensely. But very modern critics need not be so intensely bored. There is something very lovely about the good impressionist pictures. And ten years hence critics will be bored by the present run of post-impressionists, though not so passionately bored, for these post-impressionists don't move us as the impressionists moved our fathers. We have to persuade ourselves, and we have to persuade one another to be impressed by the post-impressionists, on the whole. On the whole, they rather depress us. Which is perhaps good for us.

But modern art criticism is in a curious hole. Art has suddenly gone into rebellion, against all the canons of accepted religion, accepted good form, accepted everything. When the cat came back from the delicious impressionist excursion, it came back rather tattered, but bristling and with its claws out. The glorious escape was all an illusion. There *was* substance still in the world, a thousand times be damned to it! There *was* the body, the great lumpy body. There it was; you had it shoved down your throat. What really existed was lumps, lumps. Then paint 'em. Or else paint the thin 'spirit' with gaps in it and looking merely dishevelled and 'found out'. Paint had found the spirit out.

This is the sulky and rebellious mood of the post-impressionists. They still hate the body—hate it. But in a rage they admit its existence, and paint it as huge lumps, tubes, cubes, planes, volumes, spheres, cones, cylinders, all the 'pure' or mathematical forms of substance. As for landscape, it comes in for some of the same rage. It has also suddenly gone lumpy. Instead of being nice and ethereal and non-sensual, it was discovered by Van Gogh to be heavily, overwhelmingly substantial and sensual. Van Gogh took up landscape in heavy spadefuls. And Cézanne had to admit it. Landscape, too, after being, since Claude Lorraine, a thing of pure luminosity and floating shadows, suddenly exploded, and came tumbling back on to the canvases of artists in lumps. With Cézanne landscape 'crystallized', to use one of the favourite terms of the critics, and it has gone on crystallizing into cubes, cones, pyramids and soforth ever since.

The impressionists brought the world at length, after centuries of effort, into the delicious oneness of light. At last, at last! Hail, Holy Light! the great natural One, the universal, the universalizer! We are not divided, all one body we—one in Light, lovely light! No sooner had this pæan gone up than the post-impressionists, like Judas, gave the show away. They exploded the illusion, which fell back to the canvas of art in a chaos of lumps.

This new chaos, of course, needed new apologists who therefore rose up in hordes to apologize, almost, for the new chaos. They felt a little guilty about it, so they took on new notes of effrontery, defiant as any Primitive Methodists, which indeed they are: the Primitive Methodists of art criticism. These evangelical gentlemen at once ran up their chapels, in a Romanesque or Byzantine shape, as was natural for a primitive and a methodist, and started to cry forth their doctrines in the decadent wilderness. They discovered once more that the æsthetic experience was an ecstasy, an ecstasy granted only to the chosen few, the elect, among whom the said critics were, of course, the arch-elect. This was outdoing Ruskin. It was almost Calvin come to art. But let scoffers scoff, the æsthetic ecstasy was vouchsafed only to the few, the elect, and even then, only when they had freed their minds of false doctrine. They had renounced the mammon of 'subject' in pictures, they went whoring no more after the Babylon of painted 'interest', nor did they hanker after the flesh-pots of artistic 'representation'. Oh, purify yourselves, ye who would know the æsthetic ecstasy, and be lifted up to the 'white peaks of artistic inspiration'. Purify yourselves of all base hankering for a tale that is told, and of all low lust for likenesses. Purify yourselves, and know the one supreme way, the way of Significant Form. I am the revelation and the way! I am Significant Form, and my unutterable name is Reality. Lo, I am Form and I am Pure, behold I am Pure Form. I am the revelation of Spiritual Life, moving behind the veil. I come forth and make myself known, and I am Pure Form, behold I am Significant Form.

So the prophets of the new era in art cry aloud to the multitude, in exactly the jargon of the revivalists, for revivalists they are. They will revive the Primitive-Method brethren, the Byzantines, the Ravennese, the early Italian and French primitives (which ones, in particular, we aren't told): these were Right, these were Pure, these were Spiritual, these were Real! and the builders of early Romanesque churches, Oh, my brethren! these were holy men, before the world went a-whoring after Gothic. Oh, return, my brethren, to the Primitive Method, lift up your eyes to Significant Form and be saved——

Now myself, brought up as a Nonconformist as I was, I just was never able to understand the language of salvation. I never knew what they were talking about, when they raved about being saved, and safe in the arms of Jesus, and Abraham's bosom, and seeing the great light, and entering into glory: I just was puzzled, for what did it *mean*? It seemed to work out as a getting rather drunk on your own self-importance, and afterwards coming dismally sober again and being rather unpleasant. That was all I could see in actual experience of the entering-into-glory business. The term itself, like something which ought to mean something but somehow doesn't, stuck on my mind like an irritating burr, till I decided that it was just an artificial stimulant to the individual

93

self-conceit. How could I enter into glory, when glory is just an abstraction of a human state, and not a separate reality at all? If glory means anything at all, it means the thrill a man gets when a great many people look up to him with mixed awe, reverence, delight. To-day, it means Rudolf Valentino. So that the cant about entering into glory is just used fuzzily to enhance the individual sense of self-importance—one of the rather cheap cocaine-phrases.

And I'm afraid 'æsthetic ecstasy' sounds to me very much the same, especially when accompanied by exhortations. It sounds like another great uplift into self-importance, another apotheosis of personal conceit: especially when accompanied by a lot of jargon about the pure world of reality existing behind the veil of this vulgar world of accepted appearances, and of the entry of the elect through the doorway of visual art. Too evangelical altogether, too much chapel and Primitive Methodist, too obvious a trick for advertising one's own self-glorification. The ego, as an American says, shuts itself up and paints the inside of the walls sky-blue, and thinks it is in heaven.

And then the great symbols of this salvation. When the evangelical says: Behold the lamb of God?—what on earth does he want one to behold? Are we invited to look at a lamb, with woolly, muttony appearance, frisking and making its little pills? Awfully nice, but what *has* it got to do with God or my soul? Or the cross? What *do* they expect us to see in the cross? A sort of gallows? Or the mark we use to cancel a mistake? Cross it out! That the cross by itself was supposed to *mean* something always mystified me. The same with the Blood of the Lamb. Washed in the Blood of the Lamb! always seemed to me an extremely unpleasant suggestion. And when Jerome says: He who has once washed in the blood of Jesus need never wash again!—I feel like taking a hot bath at once, to wash off even the suggestion.

And I find myself equally mystified by the cant phrases like Significant Form and Pure Form. They are as mysterious to me as the Cross and the Blood of the Lamb. They are just the magic jargon of invocation, nothing else. If you want to invoke an æsthetic ecstasy, stand in front of a Matisse and whisper fervently under your breath, 'Significant Form! Significant Form!' and it will come. It sounds to me like a form of masturbation, an attempt to make the body react to some cerebral formula.

No, I am afraid modern criticism has done altogether too much for modern art. If painting survives this outburst of ecstatic evangelicism, which it will, it is because people do come to their senses, even after the silliest vogue.

And so we can return to modern French painting, without having to quake before the bogey, or the Holy Ghost of Significant Form: a bogey which doesn't exist if we don't mind leaving aside our self-importance when we look at a picture.

The actual fact is that in Cézanne modern French art made its first tiny step back to real substance, to objective substance, if we may call it so. Van Gogh's earth was still subjective earth, himself projected into the earth. But Cézanne's apples are a real attempt to let the apple exist in its own separate entity, without transfusing it with personal emotion. Cézanne's great effort was, as it were, to shove the apple away from him, and let it live of itself. It seems a small thing to do; yet it is the first real sign that man has made for several thousands of years that he is willing to admit that matter *actually* exists. Strange as it may seem, for thousands of years, in short, ever since the mythological 'Fall', man has been preoccupied with the constant preoccupation of the denial of the existence of matter, and the proof that matter is only a form of spirit. And then, the moment it is done, and we realize finally that matter is only a form of energy, whatever that may be, in the same instant matter rises up and hits us over the head and makes us realize that it exists absolutely, since it is compact energy itself.

Cézanne felt it in paint, when he felt for the apple. Suddenly he felt the tyranny of mind, the white, worn-out arrogance of the spirit, the mental consciousness, the enclosed ego in its sky-blue heaven self-painted. He felt the sky-blue prison. And a great conflict started inside him. He was dominated by his old mental consciousness, but he wanted terribly to escape the domination. He wanted to *express* what he suddenly, convulsedly knew: the existence of matter. He terribly wanted to paint the real existence of the body, to make it artistically palpable. But he couldn't. He hadn't got there yet. And it was the torture of his life. He wanted to be himself in his own procreative body —and he couldn't. He was, like all the rest of us, so intensely and exclusively a mental creature, or a spiritual creature, or an egoist, that he could no longer identify himself with his phallus. He wanted to, terribly. At first he determined to do it by sheer bravado and braggadocio. But no good; it couldn't be done that way. He had, as one critic says, to become humble. But it wasn't a question of becoming humble. It was a question of abandoning his cerebral conceit and his 'willed ambition', and coming down to brass tacks. Poor Cézanne, there he is in his self-portraits, even the early showy ones, peeping out like a mouse and saying: I *am* a man of flesh, am I not?—for he was not quite, as none of us are. The man of flesh has been slowly destroyed through centuries, to give place to the man of spirit, the mental man, the ego, the self-conscious I. And in his artistic soul, Cézanne knew it, and wanted to rise in the flesh. He couldn't do it, and it embittered him. Yet, with his apple, he did shove the stone from the door of the tomb.

He wanted to be a man of flesh, a real man: to get out of the sky-blue prison into real air. He wanted to live, really live in the body, to know the world through his instincts and his intuitions, and to be himself in his procreative blood, not in his mere mind and spirit. He wanted it, he wanted it terribly. And whenever he tried, his mental consciousness, like a cheap fiend, interfered. If he wanted to paint a woman, his mental consciousness simply overpowered him and wouldn't let him paint the woman of flesh, the first Eve who lived before any of the fig-leaf nonsense. He couldn't do it. If he wanted to paint people, intuitively and instinctively, he couldn't do it. His mental concept shoved in front, and he *wouldn't* paint *them*—mere representations of what the *mind* accepts, not what the intuitions gather—and they, his mental concepts, wouldn't let him paint them from intuition;

they shoved in between all the time, so he painted his conflict and his failure, and the result is almost ridiculous.

Woman he was not allowed to know by intuition; his mental self, his ego, that bloodless fiend, forbade him. Man, other men he was likewise not allowed to know—except by a few, few touches. The earth likewise he was not allowed to know: his landscapes are mostly acts of rebellion against the mental concept of landscape. After a fight tooth-and-nail for forty years, he did succeed in knowing an apple, fully; and, not quite so fully, a jug or two. That was all he achieved.

It seems little, and he died embittered. But it is the first step that counts, and Cézanne's apple is a great deal, more than Plato's Idea. Cézanne's apple rolled the stone from the mouth of the tomb, and if poor Cézanne couldn't unwind himself from his cerements and mental winding-sheet, but had to lie still in the tomb, till he died, still he gave us a chance.

The history of our era is the nauseating and repulsive history of the crucifixion of the procreative body for the glorification of the spirit, the mental consciousness. Plato was an arch-priest of this crucifixion. Art, that handmaid, humbly and honestly served the vile deed, through three thousand years at least. The Renaissance put the spear through the side of the already crucified body, and syphilis put poison into the wound made by the imaginative spear. It took still three hundred years for the body to finish: but in the eighteenth century it became a corpse, a corpse with an abnormally active mind: and to-day it stinketh.

We, dear reader, you and I, we were born corpses, and we are corpses. I doubt if there is even one of us who has even known so much as an apple, a whole apple. All we know is shadows, even of apples. Shadows of everything, of the whole world, shadows even of ourselves. We are inside the tomb, and the tomb is wide and shadowy like hell, even if sky-blue by optimistic paint, so we think it is all the world. But our world is a wide tomb full of ghosts, replicas. We are all spectres, we have not been able to touch even so much as an apple. Spectres we are to one another. Spectre you are to me, spectre I am to you. Shadow you are even to yourself. And by shadow I mean idea, concept, the abstracted reality, the ego. We are not solid. We don't live in the flesh. Our instincts and intuitions are dead, we live wound round with the winding-sheet of abstraction. And the touch of anything solid hurts us. For our instincts and intuitions, which are our feelers of touch and knowing through touch, they are dead, amputated. We walk and talk and eat and copulate and laugh and evacuate wrapped in our winding-sheets, all the time wrapped in our winding-sheets.

So that Cézanne's apple hurts. It made people shout with pain. And it was not till his followers had turned him again into an abstraction that he was ever accepted. Then the critics stepped forth and abstracted his good apple into Significant Form, and henceforth Cézanne was saved. Saved for democracy. Put safely in the tomb again, and the stone rolled back. The resurrection was postponed once more.

As the resurrection will be postponed *ad infinitum* by the good bourgeois corpses in their cultured winding-sheets. They will run up a chapel to the risen body, even if it is only an apple, and kill it on the spot. They are wide-awake, are the corpses, on the alert. And a poor mouse of a Cézanne is alone in the years. Who else shows a spark of awakening life, in our marvellously civilized cemetery? All is dead, and dead breath preaching with phosphorescent effulgence about æsthetic ecstasy and Significant Form. If only the dead would bury their dead. But the dead are not dead for nothing. Who buries his own sort? The dead are cunning and alert to pounce on any spark of life and bury it, even as they have already buried Cézanne's apple and put up to it a white tombstone of Significant Form.

For who of Cézanne's followers does anything but follow at the triumphant funeral of Cézanne's achievement? They follow him in order to bury him, and they succeed. Cézanne is deeply buried under all the Matisses and Vlamincks of his following, while the critics read the funeral homily.

It is quite easy to accept Matisse and Vlaminck and Friecsy and all the rest. They are just Cézanne abstracted again. They are all just tricksters, even if clever ones. They are all mental, mental, egoists, egoists, egoists. And therefore they are all acceptable now to the enlightened corpses of connoisseurs. You needn't be afraid of Matisse and Vlaminck and the rest. They will never give your corpse-anatomy a jar. They are just shadows, minds, mountebanking and playing charades on canvas. They may be quite amusing charades, and I am all for the mountebank. But of course it is all games inside the cemetery, played by corpses and *hommes d'esprit*, even *femmes d'esprit*, like Mademoiselle Laurencin. As for *l'esprit*, said Cézanne, I don't give a fact for it. Perhaps not! But the connoisseur will give large sums of money. Trust the dead to pay for their amusement, when the amusement is deadly!

The most interesting figure in modern art, and the only really interesting figure, is Cézanne: and that not so much because of his achievement as because of his struggle. Cézanne was born at Aix in Provence in 1839: small, timorous, yet sometimes bantam defiant, sensitive, full of grand ambition, yet ruled still deeper by a naïve, Mediterranean sense of truth or reality, imaginative, call it what you will. He is not a big figure. Yet his struggle is truly heroic. He was a bourgeois, and one must never forget it. He had a moderate bourgeois income. But a bourgeois in Provence is much more real and human than a bourgeois in Normandy. He is much nearer the actual people, and the actual people are much less subdued by awe of his respectable bourgeois money.

Cézanne was naïf to a degree, but not a fool. He was rather insignificant, and grandeur impressed him terribly. Yet still stronger in him was the little flame of life where he *felt* things to be true. He didn't betray himself in order to get success, because he couldn't: to his nature it was impossible: he was too pure to be able to betray his own small real flame for immediate rewards. Perhaps that is the best one can say of a man, and it puts Cézanne —small and insignificant as he is—among the heroes. He would *not* abandon his own vital imagination.

He was terribly impressed by physical splendour

and flamboyancy, as people usually are in the lands of the sun. He admired terribly the splendid virtuosity of Paul Veronese and Tintoretto, and even of later and less good baroque painters. He wanted to be like that—terribly he wanted it. And he tried very, very hard, with bitter effort. And he always failed. It is a cant phrase with the critics to say 'he couldn't draw'. Mr. Fry says: 'With all his rare endowments, he happened to lack the comparatively common gift of illustration, the gift that any draughtsman for the illustrated papers learns in a school of commercial art.'

Now this sentence gives away at once the hollowness of modern criticism. In the first place, can one learn a 'gift' in a school of commercial art, or anywhere else? A gift surely is given, we tacitly assume by God or Nature or whatever higher power we hold responsible for the things we have no choice in.

Was then Cézanne devoid of this gift? Was he simply incapable of drawing a cat so that it would look like a cat? Nonsense! Cézanne's work is full of accurate drawing. His more trivial pictures, suggesting copies from other masters, are perfectly well drawn—that is, conventionally: so are some of the landscapes, so even is that portrait of M. Geffroy and his books, which is, or was so famous. Why these cant phrases about not being able to draw? Of course Cézanne could draw, as well as anybody else. And he had learned everything that was necessary in the art schools.

He *could* draw. And yet, in his terrifically earnest compositions in the late Renaissance or baroque manner, he drew so badly. Why? Not because he couldn't. And not because he was sacrificing 'significant form' to 'insignificant form', or mere slick representation, which is apparently what artists themselves mean when they talk about drawing. Cézanne knew all about drawing: and he surely knew as much as his critics do about significant form. Yet he neither succeeded in drawing so that things looked right, nor combining his shapes so that he achieved real form. He just failed.

He failed, where one of his little slick successors would have succeeded with one eye shut. And why? Why did Cézanne fail in his early pictures? Answer that, and you'll know a little better what art is. He didn't fail because he understood nothing about drawing or significant form or æsthetic ecstasy: he knew about them all, and didn't give a spit for them.

Cézanne failed in his earlier pictures because he was trying with his mental consciousness to do something which his living provençal body didn't want to do, or couldn't do. He terribly wanted to do something grand and voluptuous and sensuously satisfying, in the Tintoretto manner. Mr. Fry calls that his 'willed ambition', which is a good phrase, and says he had to learn humility, which is a bad phrase.

The 'willed ambition' was more than a mere willed ambition—it was a genuine desire. But it was a desire that thought it could be satisfied by ready-made baroque expressions, whereas it needed to achieve a whole new marriage of mind and matter. If we believed in reincarnation, then we should have to believe that after a certain number of new incarnations into the body of an artist, the soul of Cézanne *would* produce grand and voluptuous and sensually rich pictures—but not at all

108

in the baroque manner. Because the pictures he actually did produce with undeniable success are the first steps in that direction, sensual and rich, with not the slightest hint of baroque, but new, the man's new grasp of substantial reality.

There was, then, a certain discrepancy between Cézanne's *notion* of what he wanted to produce, and his other, intuitive knowledge of what he *could* produce. For whereas the mind works in possibilities, the intuitions work in actualities, and what you *intuitively* desire, that is possible to you. Whereas what you mentally or 'consciously' desire is nine times out of ten impossible: hitch your wagon to a star, and you'll just stay where you are.

So the conflict, as usual, was not between the artist and his medium, but between the artist's *mind* and the artist's *intuition* and *instinct*. And what Cézanne had to learn was not humility—cant word!—but honesty, honesty with himself. It was not a question of any gifts of significant form or æsthetic ecstasy: it was a question of Cézanne being himself, just Cézanne. And when Cézanne is himself he is not Tintoretto nor Veronese nor anything baroque at all. Yet he is something *physical*, and even sensual: qualities which he had identified with the masters of virtuosity.

In passing, if we think of Henri Matisse, a real virtuoso, and imagine him possessed with a 'willed ambition' to paint grand and flamboyant baroque pictures, then we know at once that he would not have to 'humble' himself at all, but that he would start in and paint with great success grand and flamboyant modern-baroque pictures. He would succeed because he has the gift of virtuosity. And the gift of virtuosity simply means that you don't have to humble yourself, or even be honest with yourself, because you are a clever mental creature who is capable at will of making the intuitions and instincts subserve some mental concept: in short, you can prostitute your body to your mind, your instincts and intuitions you can prostitute to your 'willed ambition', in a sort of masturbation process, and you can produce the impotent glories of virtuosity. But Veronese and Tintoretto are real painters, they are not mere *virtuosi*, as some of the later men are.

The point is very important. Any creative act occupies the whole consciousness of a man. This is true of the great discoveries of science as well as of art. The truly great discoveries of science and real works of art are made by the whole consciousness of man working together in unison and oneness; instinct, intuition, mind, intellect all fused into one complete consciousness, and grasping what we may call a complete truth, or a complete vision, a complete revelation in sound. A discovery, artistic or otherwise, may be more or less intuitional, more or less mental; but intuition will have entered into it, and mind will have entered too. The whole consciousness is concerned, in every case. And a painting requires the activity of the whole imagination, for it is made of imagery, and the imagination is that form of complete consciousness in which predominates the intuitive awareness of forms, images, or *physical* awareness.

And the same applies to the genuine appreciation of a work of art, or the *grasp* of a scientific law, as to the production of the same. The whole consciousness is occupied, not merely the mind alone, or merely the body. The mind and spirit alone can never really grasp a work of art, though they may, in a masturbating fashion, provoke the body into an ecstasized response. The ecstasy will die out into ash and more ash. And the reason we have so many trivial scientists promulgating fantastic 'facts' is that so many modern scientists likewise work with the mind alone, and *force* the intuitions and instincts into a prostituted acquiescence. The very statement that water is H_2O is a mental *tour de force*. With our bodies we know that water is *not* H_2O, our intuitions and instincts both know it is not so. But they are bullied by the impudent mind. Whereas if we said that water, under certain circumstances, produces two volumes of hydrogen and one of oxygen, then the intuitions and instincts would agree entirely. But that water *is composed* of two volumes of hydrogen to one of oxygen we cannot physically believe. It needs something else. Something is missing.

A parallel case is all this modern stuff about astronomy, stars, their distances and speeds and so on, talking of billions and trillions of miles and years and so forth: it is just occult. The mind is revelling in words, the intuitions and instincts are just left out, or prostituted into a sort of ecstasy. In fact the sort of ecstasy that lies in absurd figures such as 2,000,000,000,000,000,000,000,000,000,000 miles or years or tons, figures which abound in modern *scientific* books on astronomy, is just the sort of æsthetic ecstasy that the over-mental critics of art assert they experience to-day from Matisse's pictures. It is all poppy-cock. The body is either stunned to a corpse, or prostituted to ridiculous thrills, or stands coldly apart.

When I read how far off the suns are, and what they are made of, and so on, and so on, I believe all I am *able* to believe, with the true imagination. But when my intuition and instinct can grasp no more, then I call my mind to a halt. I am not going to accept mere mental asseverations. The mind can assert anything, and pretend it has proved it. My beliefs I test on my body, on my intuitional consciousness, and when I get a response there, then I accept. The same is true of great scientific 'laws' like the law of evolution. After years of acceptance of the 'laws' of evolution—rather desultory or 'humble' acceptance—now I realize that my vital imagination makes great reservations. I find I can't, with the best will in the world, believe that the species have 'evolved' from one common life-form. I just can't feel it, I have to violate my intuitive and instinctive awareness of something else, to make myself believe it. But since I know that my intuitions and instincts may still be held back by prejudice, I seek in the world for someone to make me intuitively and instinctively feel the truth of the 'law'—and I don't find anybody. I find scientists, just like artists, asserting things they are *mentally* sure of, in fact cocksure, but about which they are much too egoistic and ranting to be *intuitively, instinctively* sure. When I find a man, or a woman, intuitively and instinctively sure of anything I am all respect. But for scientific or artistic braggarts how can one have respect? The intrusion of the egoistic element is a sure proof of intuitive uncertainty. No man who is sure by instinct and intuition *brags*, though he may fight tooth-and-nail for his beliefs.

Which brings us back to Cézanne, why he couldn't draw, or why he couldn't paint baroque masterpieces. It is just because he was real, and could only believe in his own expression when it expressed a moment of wholeness or completeness of consciousness in himself. He could not prostitute one part of himself to the other. He *could* not masturbate, in paint or words. And that is saying a very great deal, to-day; to-day, the great day of the masturbating consciousness, when the mind prostitutes the sensitive, responsive body, and just forces the reactions. The masturbating consciousness produces all kinds of novelties, which thrill for the moment, then go very dead. It cannot produce a single genuinely new utterance.

What we have to thank Cézanne for is not his humility, but for his proud, high spirit that refused to accept the glib utterances of his facile mental self. He wasn't poor-spirited enough to be facile— nor humble enough to be satisfied with visual and emotional clichés. Thrilling as the baroque masters were to him in themselves, he realized that as soon as he reproduced them, he produced nothing but cliché. The mind is full of all sorts of memory, visual, tactile, emotional memory, memories, groups of memories, systems of memories. A cliché is just a worn-out memory that has no more emotional or intuitional root, and has become a habit. Whereas a novelty is just a new grouping of clichés, a new arrangement of accustomed memories. That is why a novelty is so easily accepted: it gives the little shock or thrill of surprise, but it does not *disturb* the emotional and intuitive self. It forces you to see nothing new, it is only a novel compound of clichés. The work of most of Cézanne's successors is just novel, just a new arrangement of clichés, soon growing stale. And the clichés are Cézanne-clichés, just as in Cézanne's own earlier pictures his clichés were all, or mostly, baroque-clichés.

Cézanne's early history as a painter is a history of his fight with his own cliché. His consciousness wanted a new realization. And his ready-made mind offered him all the time a ready-made expression. And Cézanne, far too inwardly proud and haughty to accept the ready-made clichés that came from his mental consciousness, stocked with memories, and which appeared mocking at him on his canvas, spent most of his time smashing his own forms to bits. To a true artist, and to the living imagination, the cliché is the deadly enemy. Cézanne had a bitter fight with it. He hammered it to pieces a thousand times. And still it reappeared.

Now again we can see why Cézanne's drawing was so bad. It was bad because it represented a smashed, mauled cliché, terribly knocked about. If Cézanne had been willing to accept his own baroque cliché, his drawing would have been perfectly conventionally 'all right', and not a critic would have had a word to say about it. But when his drawing was conventionally all right, to Cézanne himself it was mockingly all wrong, it was cliché. So he flew at it and knocked all the shape and stuffing out of it, and when it was so mauled that it was all wrong, and he was exhausted with it, he let it go; bitterly, because it still was not what he wanted. And here comes in the comic element in Cézanne's pictures. His rage with the cliché made him distort the cliché sometimes into parody as we see in pictures like *The Pasha* and *La Femme*. 'You *will* be cliché, will you?' he gnashes. 'Then *be* it!' And he shoves it in a frenzy of exasperation over into parody. And the sheer exasperation makes the parody still funny; but the laugh is a little on the wrong side of the face.

This smashing of the cliché lasted a long way into Cézanne's life: indeed, it went with him to the end. The way he worked over and over his forms was his nervous manner of laying the ghost of his cliché, burying it. Then, when it disappeared perhaps from his forms themselves, it lingered in his composition, and he had to fight with the *edges* of his forms and contours, to bury the ghost there. Only his colour he knew was not cliché. He left it to his disciples to make it so.

In his very best pictures, the best of the still-life compositions, which seem to me Cézanne's greatest achievement, the fight with the cliché is still going on. But it was in the still-life pictures he learned his final method of *avoiding* the cliché: just leaving gaps through which it fell into nothingness. So he makes his landscape succeed.

In his art, all his life long, Cézanne was tangled in a twofold activity. He wanted to express something, and before he could do it, he had to fight the hydra-headed cliché, whose last head he could never lop off. The fight with the cliché is the most obvious thing in his pictures. The dust of battle rises thick, and the splinters fly wildly. And it is this dust of battle and flying of splinters which his imitators still so fervently imitate. If you give a Chinese dressmaker a dress to copy, and the dress happens to have a darned rent in it, the dressmaker carefully tears a rent in the new dress, and darns it in exact replica. And this seems to be the chief occupation of Cézanne's disciples, in every land. They absorb themselves reproducing imitation mistakes. He let off various explosions, in order to blow up the stronghold of the cliché, and his followers make grand firework imitations of the explosions, without the faintest inkling of the true attack. They do, indeed, make an onslaught on representation, true-to-life representation: because the explosion in Cézanne's pictures blew them up.

But I am convinced that what Cézanne himself wanted *was* representation. He *wanted* true-to-life representation. Only he wanted it *more* true to life. And once you have got photography, it is a very, very difficult thing to get representation *more* true-to-life: which it has to be.

Cézanne was a realist, and he wanted to be true to life. But he would not be content with the optical cliché. With the impressionists, purely optical vision perfected itself and fell *at once* into cliché, with a startling rapidity. Cézanne saw this. Artists like Courbet and Daumier were not purely optical, but the other element in these two painters, the intellectual element, was cliché. To the optical vision they added the concept of force-pressure, almost like a hydraulic brake, and this force-pressure concept is mechanical, a cliché, though still popular. And Daumier added mental satire, and Courbet added a touch of a sort of socialism, both cliché and unimaginative.

Cézanne wanted something that was neither optical nor mechanical nor intellectual. And to introduce into our world of vision something which is neither optical nor mechanical nor intellectual-psychological requires a real revolution. It was a revolution Cézanne began, but which nobody, apparently, has been able to carry on.

He wanted to touch the world of substance once more with the intuitive touch, to be aware of it with the intuitive awareness, and to express it in intuitive terms. That is, he wished to displace our present mode of mental visual consciousness, the consciousness of mental concepts, and substitute a mode of consciousness that was predominantly intuitive, the awareness of touch. In the past, the primitives painted intuitively, but *in the direction* of our present mental-visual, conceptual form of consciousness. They were working away from their own intuition. Mankind has never been able to trust the intuitive consciousness—and the decision to accept that trust marks a very great revolution in the course of human development.

Without knowing it, Cézanne, the timid little conventional man sheltering behind his wife and sister and the Jesuit father, was a pure revolutionary. When he said to his models: Be an apple!

Be an apple! he was uttering the foreword to the fall not only of Jesuits and the Christian idealists altogether, but to the collapse of our whole way of consciousness, and the substitution of another way. If the human being is going to be primarily an Apple, as for Cézanne it was, then you are going to have a new world of men: a world which has very little to say, men that can sit still and just be physically there and be truly non-moral. That was what Cézanne meant with his: 'Be an apple!' He knew perfectly well that the moment the model began to intrude her personality and her 'mind', it would be cliché, and moral, and he would have to paint cliché. The only part of her that was not banal, known *ad nauseam*, living cliché, the only part of her that was not living cliché was her appleyness. Her body, even her very sex was known, nauseously: *connu! connu!* the endless chain of known cause-and-effect, the infinite web of the hated cliché which nets us all down in utter boredom. He knew it all, he hated it all, he refused it all, this timid and 'humble' little man. He knew, as an artist, that the only bit of a woman which nowadays escapes being ready-made and ready-known cliché is the appley part of her. Oh, be an apple, and leave out all your thoughts, all your feelings, all your mind and all your soul, which we know all about and find boring beyond endurance. Leave it all out—and be an apple!—— It is the appleyness of the portrait of Cézanne's wife that makes it so permanently interesting: the appleyness, which carries with it also the feeling of knowing the other side as well, the side you don't see, the hidden side of the moon. For the intuitive apperception of the apple is so *tangibly* aware of the apple that it is aware of it *all round*, not only just of the front. The eye sees all fronts, and the mind, on the whole, is satisfied with fronts. But intuition needs all-aroundness, and instinct needs insideness. The true imagination is forever curving round to the other side, to the back of presented appearance.

So to my feeling the portraits of Madame Cézanne, particularly the portrait in the red dress, are more interesting than the portrait of M. Geffroy, or the portraits of the housekeeper or the gardener. In the same way the *Card-players* with two figures please me more than those with four.

But we have to remember, in his figure paintings, that while he was painting the appleyness he was also deliberately painting *out* the so-called humanness, the personality, the 'likeness', the physical cliché. He had deliberately to paint it out, deliberately to make the hands and face rudimentary, and so on, because if he had painted them in fully, they would have been cliché. He *never* got over the cliché denominator, the intrusion and interference of the ready-made concept, when it came to people, to men and women. Especially to women he could only give a cliché response— and that maddened him. Try as he might, woman remained a known, ready-made cliché object to him, and he *could not* break through the concepted obsession to get at the intuitive awareness of her. Except with his wife—and in his wife he did at least know the appleyness. But with his housekeeper he failed somewhat. She is a bit cliché, especially the face. So really is M. Geffroy.

With men Cézanne often dodged it by insisting

on the clothes, those stiff cloth jackets bent into thick folds, those hats, those blouses, those curtains. Some of the *Card-players*, the big ones with four figures, seem just a trifle banal, so much occupied with painted *stuff*, painted clothing, and the humanness a bit cliché. Nor good colour, nor clever composition, nor 'planes' of colour, nor anything else will save an emotional cliché from being an emotional cliché, though they may, of course, garnish it and make it more interesting.

Where Cézanne did sometimes escape the cliché altogether and really give a complete intuitive interpretation of actual objects is in some of the still-life compositions. To me, these good still-life scenes are purely representative and quite true-to-life. Here Cézanne did what he wanted to do: he made the things quite real, he didn't deliberately leave anything out, and yet he gave us a triumphant and rich intuitive vision of a few apples and kitchen pots. For once his intuitive consciousness triumphed, and broke into utterance. And here he is inimitable. His imitators imitate his accessories of tablecloths folded like tin, etc.—the unreal parts of his pictures—but they don't imitate the pots and apples, because they can't. It's the real appleyness, and you can't imitate it. Every man must create it new and different out of himself: new and different. The moment it looks 'like' Cézanne, it is nothing.

But at the same time that Cézanne was triumphing with the apple and appleyness, he was still fighting with the cliché. When he makes Madame Cézanne most *still*, most appley, he starts making the universe slip uneasily about her. It was part of his desire: to make the human form, the *life* form come to rest. Not static—on the contrary. Mobile but come to rest. And at the same time, he set the unmoving material world into motion. Walls twitch and slide, chairs bend or rear up a little, cloths curl like burning paper. Cézanne did this partly to satisfy his intuitive feeling that nothing is really *statically* at rest—a feeling he seems to have had strongly—as when he watched the lemons shrivel or go mildewed, in his still-life group, which he left lying there so long so that he *could* see that gradual flux of change: and partly to fight the cliché, which says that the inanimate world *is* static, and that walls *are* still. In his fight with the cliché, he denied that walls are still and chairs are static. In his intuitive self he *felt* for their changes.

And these two activities of his consciousness occupy his later landscapes. In the best landscapes, we are fascinated by the mysterious *shiftiness* of the scene under our eyes; it shifts about as we watch it. And we realize, with a sort of transport, how intuitively *true* this is of landscape. It is *not* still. It has its own weird anima, and to our wide-eyed perception it changes like a living animal under our gaze. This is a quality that Cézanne sometimes got marvellously.

Then again, in other pictures he seems to be saying: Landscape is not like this and not like this and not like this and not . . . etc.—and every *not* is a little blank space in the canvas, defied by the remains of an assertion. Sometimes Cézanne builds up a landscape essentially out of omissions. He puts fringes on the complicated vacuum of the cliché, so to speak, and offers us that. It is interesting in a *repudiative* fashion, but it is not the new thing. The appleyness, the intuition has gone. We have only a mental repudiation. This occupies many of the later pictures: and ecstasizes the critics.

And Cézanne was bitter. He had never, as far as his *life* went, broken through the horrible glass screen of the mental concepts, to the actual *touch* of life. In his art, he had touched the apple, and that was a great deal. He had intuitively known the apple and intuitively brought it forth on the tree of his life in paint. But when it came to anything beyond the apple, to landscape, to people, and above all to nude woman, the cliché had triumphed over him. The cliché had triumphed over him, and he was bitter, misanthropic. How not to be misanthropic, when men and women are just clichés to you, and you hate the cliché? Most people, of course, love the cliché—because most people *are* the cliché. Still, for all that, there is perhaps more appleyness in man, and even in nude woman, than Cézanne was able to get at. The cliché obtruded, so he just abstracted away from it. Those last water-colour landscapes are just abstractions from the cliché. They are blanks, with a few pearly-coloured sort of edges. The blank is vacuum, which was Cézanne's last word against the cliché. It is a vacuum. And the edges are there to assert the vacuity.

And the very fact that we can reconstruct almost instantly a whole landscape from the few indications Cézanne gives, shows what a cliché the landscape is, how it exists already, ready-made, in our minds, how it exists in a pigeon-hole of the consciousness, so to speak, and you need only be given its number to be able to get it out, complete. Cézanne's last water-colour landscapes, made up of a few touches on blank paper, are a satire on landscape altogether. *They leave so much to the imagination!*—that immortal cant phrase, which means they give you the clue to a cliché and the cliché comes. That's what the cliché exists for. And that sort of imagination is just a rag-bag memory stored with thousands and thousands of old and really worthless sketches, images, etc.— clichés.

We can see what a fight it means, the escape from the domination of the ready-made mental concept, the mental consciousness stuffed full of clichés that intervene like a complete screen between us and life. It means a long, long fight, that will probably last for ever. But Cézanne did get as far as the apple. I can think of nobody else who has done anything.

When we put it in personal terms, it is a fight in a man between his own ego, which is his ready-made mental self which inhabits either a sky-blue self-tinted heaven or a black, self-tinted hell, and his other free intuitive self. Cézanne never freed himself from his ego, in his life. He haunted the fringes of experience—'I who am so feeble in life' —but at least he knew it. At least he had the greatness to feel bitter about it. Not like the complacent bourgeois who now 'appreciate' him!

So now perhaps it is the English turn. Perhaps this is where the English will come in. They have certainly stayed out very completely. It is as if they had received the death-blow to their instinctive and intuitive bodies in the Elizabethan age, and since then they have steadily died, till now they are complete corpses. As a young English painter, an intelligent and really modest young man, said to me: But I do think we ought to begin to paint good pictures, now that we know pretty well all there is to know about how a picture should be made. You do agree, don't you, that technically we know almost all there is to know about painting?

I looked at him in amazement. It was obvious that a newborn babe was as fit to paint pictures as he was. He knew technically all there was to know about pictures: all about two-dimensional and three-dimensional composition, also the colour-dimension and the dimension of values in that view of composition which exists apart from form: all about the value of planes, the value of the angle in planes, the different values of the same colour on different planes: all about edges, visible edges, tangible edges, intangible edges: all about the nodality of form-groups, the constellating of mass-centres: all about the relativity of mass, the gravitation and the centrifugal force of masses, the resultant of the complex impinging of masses, the isolation of a mass in the line of vision: all about pattern, line pattern, edge pattern, tone pattern, colour pattern, and the pattern of moving planes: all about texture, impasto, surface, and what happens at the edge of the canvas: also which is the æsthetic centre of the canvas, the dynamic centre, the effulgent centre, the kinetic centre, the mathematical centre and the Chinese centre: also the points of departure in the foreground, and the points of disappearance in the background, together with the various routes between these points, namely, as the crow flies, as the mind intoxicated with knowledge reels and gets there; all about spotting, what you spot, which spot, on the spot, how many spots, balance of spots, recedence of spots, spots on the explosive vision and spots on the co-ordinative vision: all about literary interest and how to hide it successfully from the policeman: all about photographic representation, and which heaven it belongs to, and which hell: all about the sex-appeal of a picture, and when you can be arrested for solicitation, when for indecency: all about the psychology of a picture, which section of the mind it appeals to, which mental state it is intended to represent, how to exclude the representation of all other states of mind from the one intended, or how, on the contrary, to give a hint of complementary states of mind fringing the state of mind portrayed: all about the chemistry of colours, when to use Winsor and Newton and when not, and the relative depth of contempt to display for Lefranc on the history of colour, past and future, whether cadmium will really stand the march of ages, whether viridian will go black, blue, or merely greasy, and the effect on our great-great-grandsons of the flake white and zinc white and white lead we have so lavishly used: on the merits and demerits of leaving patches of bare, prepared canvas, and which preparation will bleach, which blacken: on the mediums to be used, the vice of linseed oil, the treachery of turps, the meanness of gums, the innocence or the unspeakable crime of varnish: on allowing your picture to be shiny, on insisting that it should be shiny, or weeping over the merest suspicion of gloss, and rubbing it with a raw potato: on brushes, and the conflicting length of the stem, the best of the hog, the length of bristle most to be desired on the many varying occasions, and whether to slash in one direction only: on the atmosphere of London, on the atmosphere of Glasgow, on the atmosphere of Rome, on the atmosphere of Paris, and the peculiar action of them all upon vermilion, cinnabar, pale cadmium yellow, mid-chrome, emerald green, veronese green, linseed oil, turps, and Lyalls's perfect medium: on quality, and the relation to light, and its ability to hold its own in so radical a change of light as that from Rome to London. All these things the young man knew—and out of it, God help him, he was going to make pictures.

Now such innocence and such naïveté, coupled with true modesty, must make us believe that we English have indeed, at least as far as paint goes, become again as little children: very little children: tiny children: babes: nay, babes unborn. And if we have really got back to the state of the unborn babe, we are perhaps almost ready to be born. The English *may* be born again, pictorially. Or, to tell the truth, they may begin for the first time to be born: since as painters of composition

134

pictures they don't really exist. They have reached the stage where their innocent egos are entirely and totally enclosed in pale blue glass bottles of insulated inexperience. Perhaps now they *must* hatch out!

'Do you think we may be on the brink of a Golden Age again, in England?' one of our most promising young writers asked me, with that same half-timorous innocence and naïveté of the young painter. I looked at him—he was a sad young man—and my eyes nearly fell out of my head. A golden age! He looked so ungolden, and though he was twenty years my junior, he felt also like my grandfather. A golden age! In England! A golden age! Now, when even money is paper! When the enclosure in the ego is final, when they are hermetically sealed and insulated from all experience, from any *touch*, from anything *solid*.

'I suppose it's up to *you*,' said I.

And he quietly accepted it.

But such innocence, such naïveté must be a prelude to something. It's a *ne plus ultra*. So why shouldn't it be a prelude to a golden age? If the innocence and naïveté as regards artistic expression doesn't become merely idiotic, why shouldn't it become golden. The young might, out of a sheer sort of mental blankness, strike the oil of their live intuition, and get a gusher. Why not? A golden gush of artistic expression! 'Now we know pretty well everything that can be known about the technical side of pictures.' A golden age! With the artists all in bottles! Bottled up!

NETTLES

NETTLES

A Rose is not a Cabbage

And still, in spite of all they do, I love the rose of
    England,
but the cabbages of England leave me cold.

Oh the cabbages of England leave me cold
even though they grow on genuine English mould,
with their caterpillars, and the care with which
    they fold
nothingness, pale nothingness in their hearts.

Now that the winter of our discontent
is settled on the land, roses are scarce in England,
    very scarce, there are none any more.
But look at the cabbages, Oh count them by the
    score!
Oh aren't they green. Oh haven't we, haven't we
    spent
a lot of money rearing them——!

Yet the cabbages of England leave me cold
no matter of what sort the cabbage be.

The Man in the Street

I met him in the street
I said: How do you do?——
He said: And who are you
when we meet?——

I sadly went my way
feeling anything but gay,
yet once more I met a man and had to stay——
    May I greet——?

He cut me very dead,
but then he turned and said:
I see you're off your head
thus to greet
in the street
a member of the British Public: don't you see
the policeman on his beat?
Well, he's there protecting *me*!——

But! said I,
but why——?

And they ran me in, to teach me why.

Britannia's Baby

Oh Britannia's got a baby, a baby, a baby
Britannia's got a baby, and she got it by and by.

It's called the British Public, the Public, the Public
It's called the British Public, including you and I.

It's such a bonny baby, a baby, a baby
It's such a bonny baby, we daren't let it cry.

So we've got a lot of nurses, of nurses, of nurses
to feed the bonny baby, and keep its tara dry.

    Eat your pap, little man, like a man!
    Drink its minky-winky, then, like a man!

    Does it want to go to bye-bye! there then, take
        its little dummy,
    take its dummy, go to bye-bye like a man,
        little man!

    Drop of whiskey in its minky? well it shall, yes
        it shall
    if it's good, if it's going to be a *good* little man.

Want to go a little tattah? so it shall, of course
    it shall
go a banging little tattah with its Auntie
if it's good!
If it's good to-day, and to-morrow-day as well
then when Sunday comes, it shall go a tattah
    with its Auntie
in a motor, in a pap-pap pap-pap motor, little
    man!

Oh isn't it a lucky little man!
to have whiskey in its minky
and to go a banging tattah with its Auntie
who loves her little man,
such a dear, kind Auntie, isn't she, to a lucky
    little man——!

For Oh, the British Public, the Public, the Public
For Oh, the British Public is a lucky little man!

Change of Government

We've got a change of government
if you know what I mean.
Auntie Maud has come to keep house
instead of Aunt Gwendoline.

They say that Auntie Maud, you know,
is rather common; she's not
so well brought up as Aunt Gwendoline is,
so perhaps she'll be more on the spot.

That's what we hope: we hope she'll be
a better manager; for Oh dear me
Aunt Gwen was a poor one! but Aunt Maud, you
     see
was brought up poor, so she'll *have* to be

more careful. Though if she's not
won't it be awful! what shall we do?
Aunt Libby's really a feeble lot,
and I simply daren't think of Aunt Lou!

I've never seen her, but they say
she's a holy terror: she takes your best frock

and *all* your best things, and just gives them away
to the char, who's as good as you are, any day.
And she makes you go to work, even if
you've got money of your own.
And she shuts you in the cellar for the least little
      tiff,
and just loves to hear you sob and groan.

Oh I do hope Aunt Maud will manage all right!
Because they say, if she doesn't
Aunt Louie is almost bound to come
with all our horrible cousins

that we've never seen, coming stamping and
      swearing
and painting the wood-work red
just to show how dangerous they are!
Oh, Aunt Louie's the one *I* dread.

The British Workman and the Government

Hold my hand, Auntie, Auntie,
Auntie, hold my hand!
I feel I'm going to be naughty, Auntie
and you don't seem to understand.

Hold my hand and love me, Auntie,
love your little boy!
We want to be loved, especially, Auntie,
us whom you can't employ.

Idle we stand at the kerb-edge, Auntie,
dangling our useless hands.
But we don't mind so much if you love us, and
    we feel
that Auntie understands.

But wages go down, and really, Auntie,
we get a pretty thin time.
But so long as we know that Auntie loves us
we'll try to act up sublime.

Hold my hand, Auntie, Auntie,
Auntie, hold my hand!
Perhaps I'm going to be naughty, Auntie
and you don't seem to understand.

Clydesider

If Maudie doesn't love us
then why should we be good?
Why shouldn't we steal the jam in the cupboard
and all the dainty food

as we never get a taste of! really
it ought all to be Jock's and mine.
Maudie is nought but the housekeeper
and she kens it fine.

So if Maudie doesn't suit us
she's got to pack and go.
We're getting to be big lads now, an' soon
we can run our own show.

Flapper Vote

We voted 'em in, and we'll vote 'em out!
We'll show 'em a thing or two, never you doubt.

Lizzie and Lucy and me and Flossie
we'll show these old uncles who's going to be bossy!

Now then, Prime Minister, hold on a bit!
Remember who voted you into your seat!

But for Lizzie and Lucy and Flossie and me
you all of you know where you'd jolly well be.

But me and Lucy and Flossie and Lizzie
we thought we'd elect you to keep you all busy.

So be a nice uncle, be good to us girls;
just vote us some pin-money, to encourage our
    curls!

And Lizzie and me and Flossie and Lucy
we'll back you up, uncle! We're young, and we're
    juicy!——

SONGS I LEARNT AT SCHOOL

1. Neptune's Little Affair with Freedom

Father Neptune one day to Freedom did say:
If ever I lived upon dry—y land,
The spot I should hit on would be little Britain——
Said Freedom: Why that's my own I—sland!——

> *'Oh what a bright little I—sland!*
> *A right little, tight little I—sland!*
> *Seek all the world round there's none can be found*
> *So happy as our little I—sland!'*

So Father Neptune walked up the shore
bright and naked aft and fore
as he's always been, since the Flood and before.

And instantly rose a great uproar
of Freedom shrieking till her throat was sore:
Arrest him, he's indecent, he's obscene what's
    more!——

Policemen and the British nation
threw themselves on him in indignation
with handcuffs, and took him to the police-station

The sea-god said, in consternation:
But I came at Freedom's invitation!——
So then they charged him with defamation.

And all the sea-nymphs out at sea
rocked on the waves and sang lustily
thinking old Neptune was off on a spree
with giddy Freedom in the land of the Free:

> '*Oh what a bright little I—sland!*
> *A right little, tight little I—sland!*——'

2. My Native Land

First verse:

Of every land or east or west
I love my native land the best, etc. etc.

Second verse:

Of every tongue or east or west
I love my native tongue the best
Though not so smoothly spoken,
Nor woven with Italian art
Yet when it speaks from heart to heart
The spell is never broken
The—e spell is—s never bro—o—ken!

Oh a man may travel both east and west
and still speak his native language the best.

But don't try it on, Oh never start
this business of speaking from heart to heart
in mother English, or you're in the cart.

For our honest and healthy English tongue
is apt to prove a great deal too strong

for our dainty, our delicate English ears.
Oh touch the harp, touch the harp gently, my
    dears!

We English are so sensitive, much more than
    appears——

Oh don't for an instant ever dream
of speaking plain English to an Englishman; you'll
    seem

to him worse than a bolshevist Jew, or an utter
outsider sprung up from some horrible gutter.

Oh mince your words, and mince them well
if you don't want to break the sweet English spell.

For we English are really a race apart,
superior to everyone else: so don't start

being crude and straightforward, you'll only prove
you're a rank outsider of the fifth remove.

3. The British Boy

First verse:

> Oh I'm a British bo—oy, Sir,
> A joy to—o tell it you.
> God make me of it worthy
> Life's toilsome journey through!
> And when to man's estate I grow
> My British blood the world shall know,
> For I'm a British bo—oy, Sir.
> A joy to—o tell it you!——

And so to man's estate he grew
and his British blood the world it knew.

And the world it didn't give a hoot
if his blood was British or Timbuctoot.

But with that British blood of his
he painted some pictures, real beauties

he thought them, so he sent them home
to Britain, where his blood came from.

But Britannia turned pale, and began to faint
—Destroy, she moaned, these horrors in paint!·

He answered: Dear Britannia, why?
I'm your British boy, and I did but try——!

If my pictures are nude, so once were you,
and you will be again, therefore why look blue!——

Britannia hid behind her shield
lest her heel of Achilles should be revealed,

and she said: Don't dare, you wretch, to be lewd!
I never was nor will be nude!——

And she jabbed her British trident clean
through the poor boy's pictures: You see what I
        mean!——

But the British boy he turned and fled
for the trident was levelled at his head.

Henceforth he'll keep clear of her toasting-fork.
Pleasing Britannia is no light work.

154

13,000 People

Thirteen thousand people came to see
my pictures, eager as the honey bee

for the flowers; and I'll tell you what
all eyes sought the same old spot

in every picture, every time,
and gazed and gloated without rhyme

or reason, where the leaf should be,
the fig-leaf that was not, woe is me!

And they blushed, they giggled, they sniggered,
    they leered,
or they boiled and they fumed, in fury they sneered

and said: Oh boy, I tell you what,
look at that one there, that's pretty hot!——

And they stared and they stared, the half-witted lot
at the spot where the fig-leaf just was not!

But why, I ask you? Oh tell me why?
Aren't they made quite the same, then, as you
    and I?

Can it be they've been trimmed, so they've never
  seen

the innocent member that a fig-leaf will screen?

What's the matter with them? aren't they women
  and men?

or is something missing? or what's wrong with
  them then?

that they stared and leered at the single spot
where a fig-leaf might have been, and was not.

I thought it was a commonplace
that a man or a woman in a state of grace

in puris naturalibus, don't you see,
had normal pudenda, like you and me.

But it can't be so, for they behaved
like lunatics looking, they bubbled and raved

or gloated or peeped at the simple spot
where a fig-leaf might have been, but was not.

I tell you, there must be something wrong
with my fellow-countrymen; or else I don't belong.

156

Innocent England

Oh what a pity, Oh! don't you agree
that figs aren't found in the land of the free!

Fig-trees don't grow in my native land;
there's never a fig-leaf near at hand

when you want one; so I did without;
and that is what the row's about.

Virginal, pure policemen came
and hid their faces for very shame,

while they carried the shameless things away
to gaol, to be hid from the light of day.

And Mr. Mead, that old, old lily
said: 'Gross! coarse! hideous!'—and I, like a silly

thought he meant the faces of the police-court
　　officials,
and how right he was, and I signed my initials

to confirm what he said: but alas, he meant
my pictures, and on the proceedings went.

The upshot was, my pictures must burn
that English artists might finally learn

when they painted a nude, to put a *cache sexe* on
a cache sexe, a cache sexe, or else begone!

A fig-leaf; or, if you cannot find it
a wreath of mist, with nothing behind it.

A wreath of mist is the usual thing
in the north, to hide where the turtles sing.

Though they never sing, they never sing,
don't you dare to suggest such a thing

or Mr. Mead will be after you.
—But what a pity I never knew

A wreath of English mist would do
as a cache sexe! I'd have put a whole fog.

But once and forever barks the old dog,
so my pictures are in prison, instead of in the Zoo.

Give me a Sponge

Give me a sponge and some clear, clean water
and leave me alone awhile
with my thirteen sorry pictures that have just been
    rescued
from durance vile.

Leave me alone now, for my soul is burning
as it feels the slimy taint
of all those nasty police-eyes like snail-tracks
    smearing
the gentle souls that figure in the paint.

Ah, my nice pictures, they are fouled, they are
    dirtied
not by time, but by unclean breath and eyes
of all the sordid people that have stared at them
    uncleanly
looking dirt on them, and breathing on them
    lies.

Ah my nice pictures, let me sponge you very
    gently

to sponge away the slime
that ancient eyes have left on you, where obscene
      eyes have crawled
leaving nasty films upon you every time.

Ah the clean waters of the sky, Ah! can you wash
away the evil starings and the breath
of the foul ones from my pictures? Oh purify
them now from all this touch of tainted death!

Puss-Puss!

-Oh, Auntie, isn't he a beauty! And is he a
  gentleman or a lady?
-Neither, my dear! I had him fixed. It saves him
  from so many undesirable associations.

London Mercury

Oh when Mercury came to London
they 'had him fixed'.
It saves him from so many undesirable associa
    tions.

And now all the Aunties like him so much
because, you see, he is 'neither, my dear!'

My Little Critics

My little critics must all have been brought up by
    their Aunties
who petted them, and had them fixed
to save them from undesirable associations.

It must be so. Otherwise
the sight of an ordinary Tom wouldn't send them
    into such silly hysterics,
my little critics, dear, safe little pets.

Editorial Office

Applicant for post as literary critic: Here are my credentials, Sir!——

Editor: Er—quite. But—er—biologically! Have you been fixed?—*arrangé*—you understand what I mean?

Applicant: I'm afraid I don't.

Editor (sternly): Have you been made safe for the great British Public? Has everything objectionable been removed from you?

Applicant: In what way, quite?

Editor: By surgical operation. Did your parents have you sterilized?

Applicant: I don't think so, Sir. I'm afraid not.

Editor: Good morning! Don't trouble to call again. We have the welfare of the British Public at heart.

The Great Newspaper Editor to his Subordinate

Mr. Smith, Mr. Smith
haven't I told you to take the pith
and marrow and substance out of all
the articles passing beneath your scrawl?

And now look here what you've gone and done!
You've told them that life isn't really much fun,
when you know that they've got to think that
    they're happy,

as happy as happy, Oh, so happy, you sappy.
Think of the effect on Miss Harrison
when she reads that her life isn't really much fun.
She'll take off her specs. and she'll put down the
    paper
as if it was giving off poison vapour.

And she'll avoid it; she'll go and order
The Morning Smile, sure that it will afford her
comfort and cheer, sure that it will tell her
she's a marv'lous, delicious, high-spirited feller.

You must chop up each article, make it pappy
and easy to swallow; always tell them they're
    happy,
suggest that they're spicy, yet how *pure* they are,
and what a sense of true humour they've got,
    ha-ha!

Mr. Smith, Mr. Smith
have you still to learn that pith
and marrow and substance are sure to be
indigestible to Miss Ponsonby!

Mr. Smith, Mr. Smith
if you stay in my office, you've got to be kith
and kin with Miss Jupson, whose guts are narrow
and can't pass such things as substance and
    marrow.

Mr. Smith, Mr. Smith
consider Miss Wilks, or depart forthwith.
For the British Public, once more be it said,
is summed up in a nice, narrow-gutted old maid.

Modern Prayer

Almighty Mammon, make me rich!
Make me rich quickly, with never a hitch
in my fine prosperity! Kick those in the ditch
who hinder me, Mammon, great son of a bitch

Cry of the Masses

Give us back, Oh give us back
Our bodies before we die!

Trot, trot, trot, corpse-body, to work.
Chew, chew, chew, corpse-body, at the meal.
Sit, sit, sit, corpse-body, in the car.
Stare, stare, stare, corpse-body, at the film.
Listen, listen, listen, corpse-body, to the wireless.
Talk, talk, talk, corpse-body, newspaper talk.
Sleep, sleep, sleep, corpse-body, factory-hand sleep
Die, die, die, corpse-body, doesn't matter!

Must we die, must we die
bodiless, as we lived?
Corpse-anatomies with ready-made sensations!
Corpse-anatomies, that can work.
Work, work, work,
rattle, rattle, rattle,
sit, sit, sit,
finished, finished, finished——

Ah no, Ah no! before we finally die
or see ourselves as we are, and go mad,

give us back our bodies, for a day, for a single day
to stamp the earth and feel the wind, like wakeful
    men again.
Oh, even to know the last wild wincing of despair,
aware at last that our manhood is utterly lost,
give us back our bodies for one day.

What Have They Done to You——?

What have they done to you, men of the masses
creeping back and forth to work?

What have they done to you, the saviours of the
        people?
Oh what have they saved you from?

Alas, they have saved you from yourself,
from your own body, saved you from living your
        own life.

And given you this jig-jig-jig
tick-tick-ticking of machines,
this life which is no-man's-life.

Oh a no-man's-life in a no-man's-land
this is what they've given you
in place of your own life.

The People

Ah the people, the people!
surely they are flesh of my flesh!

When, in the streets of the working quarters
they stream past, stream past, going to work;

then, when I see the iron hooked in their faces,
their poor, their fearful faces

then I scream in my soul, for I know I cannot
cut the iron hook out of their faces, that makes
    them so drawn,
nor cut the invisible wires of steel that pull them

back and forth to work,
back and forth, to work

like fearful and corpse-like fishes hooked and being
    played
by some malignant fisherman on an unseen, safe
    shore
where he does not choose to land them yet, hooked
    fishes of the factory world.

The Factory Cities

Oh, over the factory cities there seems to hover a
    doom
so dark, so dark, the mind is lost in it.

Ah, the industrial masses, with the iron hook
    through their gills,
when the evil angler has played them long enough,
another little run for their money, a few more
    turns of the reel
fixing the hook more tightly, getting it more firmly
    in——

Ah, when he begins to draw the line in tight, to
    land his fish,
the industrial masses—Ah, what will happen, what
    will happen?

Hark! the strange noise of millions of fish in panic
in panic, in rebellion, slithering millions of fish
whistling and seething and pulling the angler down
    into boiling black death!

Leaves of Grass, Flowers of Grass

Leaves of grass, what about leaves of grass?
Grass blossoms, grass has flowers, flowers of grass
dusty pollen of grass, tall grass in its midsummer
    maleness,
hay-seed and tiny grain of grass, graminiferae
not far from the lily, the considerable lily;

even the blue-grass blossoms;
even the bison knew it;
even the stupidest farmer gathers his hay in bloom,
    in blossom
just before it seeds.

Only the best matters; even the cow knows it;
grass in blossom, blossoming grass, risen to its
    height and its natural pride
in its own splendour and its own feathery maleness
the grass, the grass.

Leaves of grass, what are leaves of grass, when at
    its best grass blossoms.

Magnificent Democracy

Oh, when the grass flowers, the grass
how aristocratic it is!
Cock's-foot, fox-tail, fescue and tottering-grass
see them wave, see them wave, plumes
prouder than the Black Prince,
flowers of grass, fine men.

Oh, I am a democrat
of the grass in blossom
a blooming aristocrat all round.